Cozy Knits

50 FAST & EASY PROJECTS FROM TOP DESIGNERS

TANIS GRAY

INTERWEAVE
interweave.com

FOR GRANDMA IRENE AND GRANDMA MYRT—TWO SMART, CRAFTY WOMEN AHEAD OF THEIR TIME.

EDITOR | Michelle Bredeson

TECHNICAL EDITOR | Therese Chynoweth

ASSOCIATE ART DIRECTOR | Julia Boyles

ILLUSTRATOR | Therese Chynoweth

DESIGNER | Mae Ariola

PHOTOGRAPHER | Joe Hancock

PHOTO STYLIST | Emily Smoot

HAIR AND MAKEUP | Kathy MacKay

PRODUCTION | Katherine Jackson

Interweave
A division of F+W Media, Inc.
201 East Fourth Street
Loveland, CO 80537
interweave.com

Manufactured in China by RR Donnelley Shenzhen.

Library of Congress Cataloging-in-Publication Data
Cozy knits : 50 fast and easy projects from top designers / Tanis Gray.
    pages cm
  Includes index.
  ISBN 978-1-62033-065-4 (pbk.)
  ISBN 978-1-62033-075-3 (PDF)
1. Knitting--Patterns. I. Gray, Tanis, editor. II. Cascade Yarns.
  TT825.C729 2013
  746.43'20432--dc23
               2013012433

10 9 8 7 6 5 4 3 2 1

To locate retailers of Cascade Pacific and Pacific Chunky, go to cascadeyarns.com.

contents

introduction

As much as I enjoy the challenge of designing and knitting projects with intricate stitch patterns and elaborate construction, my first love is creating knits that are simple and fun to knit and just as much fun to wear. To put together the ultimate collection of quick and cozy projects to knit, I reached out to some of my favorite designers. The designs they created went beyond my high expectations, and I'm sure you'll feel the same.

The patterns in this book are knit in a variety of yarns from Cascade's Pacific line: Pacific, Pacific Multi, Pacific Chunky, and Pacific Chunky Multi. With versatility, value, softness, and a full spectrum of colors, this is an ideal workhorse yarn. Because it's machine washable and dryable, this superwash merino wool is perfect for knits for the whole family.

Among these fifty projects, you'll find dozens of mittens, hats, and other accessories; sumptuous sweaters, scarves, shawls, and cowls; colorful accents for the home; and lots of ideas for quick and clever gifts for everyone on your list, including little ones and the hard-to-knit-for.

All skill levels are covered in this book. Beginning knitters will find plenty of projects they can pick up and start knitting right away, while knitters who are looking to expand their stitching repertoire will learn myriad new techniques. Become an expert in slip-stitch colorwork while knitting Faina Goberstein's Ravenna Beanie or try your hand at Fair Isle knitting with Mary Jane Mucklestone's Scandinavian fingerless mitts. Learn brioche knitting with projects from Nancy Marchant and Debbie O'Neill or dip your toes into sock knitting with Lynn Wilson's ribbed slipper socks with colorwork cuffs. Whatever your interest or skill level, you'll find a healthy dose of inspiration in this jam-packed collection.

So find a comfortable spot, grab your needles, and cozy up with *Cozy Knits!*

Heartfelt Hats

Keep your noggin warm with hats for all occasions. Need a gift
in a hurry or looking for a unique chapeau to top off your look?
You'll be ahead of the game when you knit up any of the cute
and colorful toppers in this chapter.

raindrops & rivulets
CABLES AND LACE BEANIE

An eclectic mix of lazy cables and lace raindrops adorns this lovely cap. The twelve-stitch cable meanders up to the crown, where decreases are cleverly worked in among the lace stitches.

Designed by Faina Goberstein

Finished Size

18¼ (20)" (46.5 [51] cm) circumference at ribbed brim. Sample is made in size 20" (51 cm).

Yarn

Worsted weight (#4 Medium).

Shown here: Cascade Yarns *Pacific* (40% merino wool, 60% acrylic; 213 yd [195 m]/100 g): #08 baby mint, 1 skein.

Needles

Beanie: size U.S. 6 (4 mm): 16" (40 cm) circular (cir) and set of 5 double-pointed (dpn).

Brim: size U.S. 4 (3.5 mm): 16" (40 cm) circular (cir).

Adjust needle sizes if necessary to obtain the correct gauge.

Notions

Markers (m); cable needle (cn); tapestry needle.

Gauge

29½ sts and 34 rnds = 4" (10 cm) over cable patt on larger needles; 26 sts and 40 rnds = 4" (10 cm) over little leaves patt (chart B) on larger needles.

3/3 LC (3 over 3 left cross):
Sl next 3 sts onto cn and hold in front of work, k3, k3 from cn.

3/3 RC (3 over 3 right cross):
Sl next 3 sts onto cn and hold in back of work, k3, k3 from cn.

CABLE PATTERN (MULTIPLE OF 12 STS)

Rnds 1 and 2: Knit.

Rnd 3: *3/3 LC, k6; rep from * to end.

Rnds 4–6: Knit.

Rnd 7: *K6, 3/3 RC; rep from * to end.

Rnd 8: Knit.

Rep rnds 1–8 for patt.

K1, P1 RIB (EVEN NUMBER OF STS)

Rnd 1: *K1, p1; rep from * to end.

Rep rnd 1 for patt.

Beanie

BRIM

With smaller cir needle and using long-tail cast-on, CO 132 (144) sts. Place marker (pm); join for working in the rnd, being careful not to twist sts.

Work 6 rnds in k1, p1 rib.

BODY

Change to larger cir needle.

Note: Place markers after each 12-st rep to keep track of patt and initial crown decreases.

Chart A

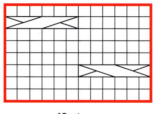

12-st rep

Work cable patt (chart A) until hat measures about 5 (5½)" (12.5 [14] cm) from beg, ending with rnd 2 or 5 of patt.

Work rnds 1–10 of little leaves patt (chart B or rnds 1–10 below); st count varies, increasing from a multiple of 6 to a multiple of 10, then decreasing back to a multiple of 6.

Rnd 1: *P5, ([k1, yo] twice, k1) into next st; rep from * to end—220 (240) sts.

Rnds 2–4: *P5, k5; rep from * to end.

Rnd 5: *P5, sl 3 tog as if to k3tog, k2tog, p3sso; rep from * to end—132 (144) sts.

Rnd 6: Purl.

Rnd 7: *P2, ([k1, yo] twice, k1) into next st, p3; rep from * to end—220 (240) sts.

Rnds 8–10: *P2, k5, p3; rep from * to end.

Chart B

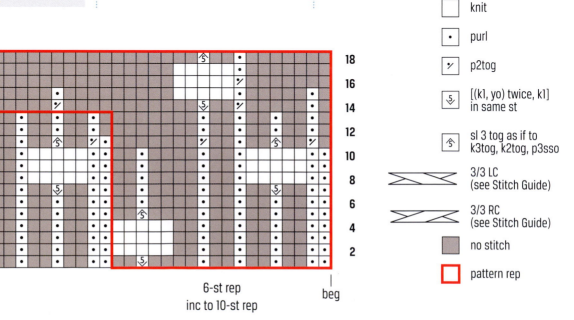

end

6-st rep
inc to 10-st rep

beg

☐	knit
•	purl
⟋	p2tog
⑤	[(k1, yo) twice, k1] in same st
⑥	sl 3 tog as if to k3tog, k2tog, p3sso
⟍⟋	3/3 LC (see Stitch Guide)
⟋⟍	3/3 RC (see Stitch Guide)
▨	no stitch
☐	pattern rep

SHAPE CROWN

Note: Change to dpn when too few sts rem to work comfortably on a cir needle.

Rnd 11 (dec): *P2tog, sl 3 tog as if to k3tog, k2tog, p3sso, p1, p2tog; rep from * to end—88 (96) sts.

Rnds 12 and 13: Purl.

Rnd 14 (dec): *P1, p2tog, ([k1, yo] twice, k1) into next st, remove marker, (p2tog) twice; rep from * to end—99 (108) sts.

Rnd 15: *P2, k5, p2; rep from * to end.

Rnd 16 (dec): *P2tog, k5, p2tog; rep from * to end—77 (84) sts.

Rnd 17: *P1, k5, p1; rep from * to end.

Rnd 18: *P1, sl 3 tog as if to k3tog, k2tog, p3sso, p1; rep from * to end—33 (36) sts rem.

Rnds 19–22: Purl.

Rnd 23 (dec): *P2tog; rep from * to last 1 (0) st, p1 (0)—17 (18) sts rem.

Cut yarn, leaving an 8" (20.5 cm) tail; thread tail through rem sts, pull tightly to close hole, fasten off on WS.

Finishing

Weave in ends.

saltwater taffy

CABLED HAT

This four-stitch cabled hat is worked from the bottom up in the round and topped with a cheeky tassel. The generous purling between the cables allows for a stretch that assures a sweet fit for all.

Designed by Kathy North

Finished Size

About 20" (51 cm) circumference (slightly stretched; hat will stretch to fit up to 23" [58.5 cm] head circumference) and 7½" (19 cm) high.

Yarn

Worsted weight (#4 Medium).

Shown here: Cascade Yarns *Pacific* (40% superwash merino, 60% acrylic; 213 yd [195 m]/100 g): #51 honeysuckle pink, 1 skein.

Needles

Size U.S. 8 (5 mm): 16" (40 cm) circular (cir).

Size U.S. 10½ (6.5 mm): 16" (40 cm) circular (cir) and set of 4 double-pointed (dpn).

Adjust needle sizes if necessary to obtain the correct gauge.

Notions

Cable needle (cn); stitch marker; tapestry needle.

Gauge

16 sts and 21 rnds = 4" (10 cm) over cable patt with 2 strands of yarn.

Note

Hat is worked in the round with 2 strands of yarn held together throughout.

Stitch Guide

2/2 RC (2 over 2 right cross): Sl next 2 sts onto cn and hold in back of work, k2, k2 from cn.

CABLE PATTERN

Rnds 1–2: *P2, k4, p2; rep from * around.

Rnd 3: *P2, 2/2 RC, p2; rep from * around.

Rnd 4: *P2, k4, p2; rep from * around.

Rep rnds 1–4 for patt.

Hat

With smaller cir needle and 2 strands of yarn, CO 80 sts. Place marker (pm), and join for working in rnds, being careful not to twist sts.

Rnds 1–4: *P2, k4, p2; rep from * around.

Change to larger cir needle.

Work cable pattern until piece measures about 6" (15 cm) from beg, ending with rnd 4.

SHAPE CROWN

Change to dpns when there are too few sts to work comfortably on cir needle.

Rnd 1 (dec): *P2tog, k4, p2tog; rep from * around—60 sts rem.

Rnd 2: *P1, k4, p1; rep from * around.

Rnd 3: *P1, 2/2 RC, p1; rep from * around.

Rnd 4: *P1, k4, p1; rep from * to last 6 sts, p1, k4, sl last st to RH needle, remove m, place slipped st on LH needle and replace m.

Rnd 5 (dec): *P2tog, k2tog twice; rep from * around—30 sts rem.

Rnd 6: *P1, k2; rep from * around.

Rnd 7 (dec): *P2tog, k1; rep from * around—20 sts rem.

Rnd 8 (dec): *K2tog; rep from * around—10 sts rem.

Cut yarn, leaving a 12" (30.5 cm) tail, thread tail through rem sts, pull tight to close hole, fasten off on WS.

Finishing

Weave in ends.

TASSEL

Cut a piece of cardboard 7" (18 cm) square. Holding 2 strands of yarn tog, wrap yarn around cardboard 10 times. Cut 2 separate pieces of yarn, one 16" (40.5 cm) long and one 24" (61 cm) long. Slip shorter strand under yarn on cardboard and tie tightly around wraps at one end of cardboard. Cut strands at opposite end. With longer rem strand, beg 1" (2.5 cm) below tied end, wrap yarn tightly around all strands a few times. Tie ends of this strand and thread tails through center of tassel. Trim ends even. Attach tassel to top of hat.

twinkle, twinkle little star

FAIR ISLE BEANIE

Large and small white stars shine on a night sky–blue background. It's not rocket science, but the irregular Fair Isle pattern will keep you on your toes.

Designed by Kathy Merrick

Finished Size

21" (53.5 cm) circumference and 7¾" (19.5 cm) high.

Yarn

Worsted weight (#4 Medium).

Shown here: Cascade Yarns *Pacific* (40% superwash merino, 60% acrylic; 213 yd [195 m]/100 g): #47 navy (MC), 1 skein; #2 white (CC), 1 skein.

Needles

Size U.S. 8 (5 mm): 16" (40 cm) circular (cir) and set of 5 double-pointed (dpn).

Adjust needle size if necessary to obtain the correct gauge.

Notions

Stitch marker (m); tapestry needle.

Gauge

18 sts and 22 rnds = 4" (10 cm) over Fair Isle chart.

Beanie

BRIM

With cir needle and 1 strand each of MC and CC held together, CO 96 sts. Place marker (pm), and join for working in rnds, taking care not to twist sts.

Rnd 1: *K1 CC, p1 MC; rep from * around.

Rnd 2: *P1 MC, k1 CC; rep from * around.

Rnd 3: Rep Rnd 1.

Work rnds 1–24 of chart, carrying yarn not in use loosely across back.

SHAPE CROWN

Change to dpn when there are too few sts to work comfortably on cir needle.

Rnd 25: Foll chart, *k2tog, k10; rep from * around—8 sts dec'd.

Rnd 26: *K2tog, k9; rep from * around—8 sts dec'd.

Rnd 27: *K2tog, k8; rep from * around—8 sts dec'd.

Rnds 28–35: Cont dec as established, with 1 fewer st in each section—8 sts rem.

Cut yarns, leaving 8" (20.5 cm) tails, thread tails through rem sts, pull tight to close hole, fasten off on WS.

Finishing

Weave in ends. Block to finished measurements.

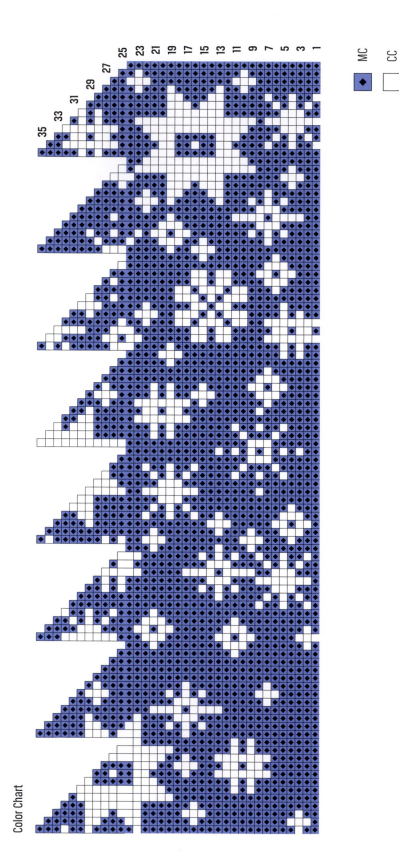

Color Chart

MC ◆
CC ☐

diamond jubilee
SLIP-STITCH HAT

Slip-stitch colorwork creates a gorgeous allover diamond pattern. Worked from the bottom up in the round starting with a simple 1x1 rib brim, this cap is sophisticated looking but simple to knit.

Designed by Faina Goberstein

Finished Sizes

17½ (19)" (44.5 [48.5] cm) circumference at ribbed brim. Shown in size 19" (48.5 cm).

Yarn

Worsted weight (#4 Medium).

Shown here: Cascade Yarns *Pacific* (40% merino wool, 60% acrylic; 213 yd [195 m]/100 g): #48 black (A), 1 skein; #15 taupe (B), 1 skein.

Needles

Hat: size U.S. 6 (4 mm): 16" (40 cm) circular (cir) and set of 5 double-pointed (dpn).

Brim: size U.S. 4 (3.5 mm): 16" (40 cm) circular (cir).

Adjust needle sizes if necessary to obtain the correct gauge.

Notions

Markers (m); tapestry needle.

Gauge

27½ sts and 46 rnds = 4" (10 cm) over mosaic stitch chart on larger needles.

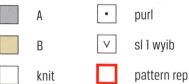
K1, P1 RIB (EVEN NUMBER OF STS)

Rnd 1: *K1, p1; rep from * to end.

Rep rnd 1 for patt.

Beanie

BRIM

With A and B, using smaller cir needle and long-tail cast-on (holding A over the thumb and B over finger), CO 120 (130) sts. Place marker (pm), and join for working in rnds, being careful not to twist sts.

Work in k1, p1 rib as foll:

With B, work 3 rnds.

With A, work 2 rnds.

With B, work 3 rnds.

With A, work 1 rnd.

With B, work 1 rnd.

BODY

Change to larger cir needle.

Note: Always slip sts with yarn in back.

Work 28 rnds of mosaic stitch chart until hat measures about 7" (18 cm) from beg, ending with rnd 10.

SHAPE CROWN

Notes: Change to dpn when too few sts rem to work comfortably on a cir needle.

Place markers after each 10-st rep to keep track of decreases.

With B:

Dec rnd 1: *K2tog, sl 1, k5, sl 1, k1; rep from * to end—108 (117) sts.

Next rnd: *P1, sl 1, p5, sl 1, p1; rep from * to end.

With A:

Dec rnd 2: *K3, (sl 1, k1) twice, k2tog; rep from * to end—96 (104) sts.

Dec rnd 3: *P2tog, (p1, sl1) twice, p2; rep from * to end—84 (91) sts.

With B:

Dec rnd 4: *Sl 1, k2tog, sl 1, ssk, sl 1; rep from * to end—60 (65) sts.

Next rnd: *(Sl 1, p1) twice, sl 1; rep from * to end.

With A:

Next rnd: *(K1, sl 1) twice, k1; rep from * to end.

Next rnd: *(P1, sl 1) twice, p1; rep from * to end.

With B:

Dec rnd 5: *Sl 1, (sl 1, k2tog, psso), sl 1; rep from * to end—36 (39) sts.

Next rnd: *Sl 1, p1, sl 1; rep from * to end.

With A:

Next rnd: Knit.

Next rnd: Purl.

Rep last 2 rnds twice more.

Dec rnd 6: *K2tog, k1; rep from * to end—24 (26) sts.

Dec rnd 7: *P2tog; rep from * to end—12 (13) sts.

Next rnd: Knit.

Cut yarn, leaving an 8" (20.5 cm) tail, thread tail through rem sts, pull tightly to close hole, fasten securely on WS.

Finishing

Weave in ends.

Mosaic-Stitch Chart

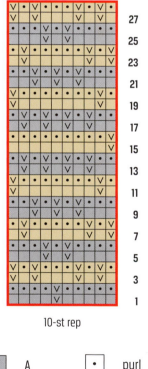

10-st rep

A (gray)	• purl
B (tan)	V sl 1 wyib
knit	▭ pattern rep

i-cord, can you?
SPIRAL BEANIE

This swirly sensation is knit almost entirely out of I-cord. Worked from the top down and assembled as you go to form a circle, it's finished off with an easy k2, p2 ribbed band. If you're a knitter looking for something different, this hat is for you!

Designed by Linda Medina

Finished Size

To fit adult woman. About 19" (48.5 cm) circumference and 8¾" (22 cm) high.

Yarn

Worsted weight (#4 Medium).

Shown here: Cascade Yarns *Pacific Multi Worsted* (40% superwash merino, 60% acrylic; 213 yd [195 m]/ 100 g): #507 lucky clover, 2 skeins.

Needles

Size U.S. 7 (4.5 mm): set of 2 double-pointed (dpn) and 16" (40 cm) circular (cir).

Adjust needle size if necessary to obtain the correct gauge.

Notions

Stitch marker; removable stitch marker; tapestry needle.

Gauge

24 sts (sts measured across 6 joined rnds) and 30 rows = 4" (10 cm) over joined I-cord.

Notes

This hat is made with an unconventional I-cord technique. It is worked from the top down in a spiral, joining the rounds as you work. Because of the number of stitches, this I-cord is more flat than round. You will always be working from the right side only. The stitches are picked up along the outer edge of the previous round, and you join the rounds as you work. A plain row is worked after each joining row.

Beanie

With dpn, CO 3 sts.

*Work 2 rows I-cord.

Next row (inc): K1f&b, k2—4 sts. Rep from * once more—5 sts.

Work 4" (10 cm) of I-cord. Tie I-cord into a loose knot close to needle. Work 2 more rows of I-cord but do not slide the sts to opposite end of dpn at end of second row.

Holding the knot upright and facing, *pick up and knit 1 st at the base of the knot, then slide sts to opposite end of needle—6 sts.

Next row: K4, skp—5 sts.

Work 1 row even but do not slide sts to opposite end of needle. Rep from * all the way around the knot, picking up sts in every row. Using removable marker, place marker (pm) in edge of piece to mark beg of rnd and move it at end of each rnd.

CROWN

*Pick up and knit 1 st in first st of next row of previous rnd, then slide sts to opposite end of needle—6 sts.

Next row: K4, skp—5 sts.

Work 1 row even but do not slide sts to opposite end of needle*. Rep from * to *, picking up sts in every row of previous rnd, and moving marker at end of each rnd, until piece measures about 3" (7.5 cm) across.

**Skip next row, pick up and knit 1 st in first st of next row of previous rnd, then slide sts to opposite end of needle—6 sts.

Next row: K4, skp, pick up and knit 1 st in first st of next row of previous rnd, then slide sts to opposite end of needle—6 sts.

Next row: K4, skp—5 sts.

Work 1 row even but do not slide sts to opposite end of needle**.

Rep from ** to ** until piece measure about 6" (15 cm) across.

SIDES

Rnd 1: Beg by picking up first st in second row of previous rnd, rep from * to *, picking up sts in every other row of previous rnd.

Rnd 2: Beg by picking up first st in first row of previous rnd, rep from * to *, picking up sts in every other row of previous rnd.

Rnds 3–6: Rep rnds 1 and 2 twice more.

Rep rnd 2 six more times; piece should measure about 7½" (19 cm) from top knot.

Rnd 13: Rep rnd 2 to last 8 rows before marker.

Next row (dec): Skip next row, pick up and knit 1 st in first st of next row of previous rnd, slide sts to opposite end of needle, k2tog, k2, skp—4 sts.

Work 1 row even but do not slide sts to opposite end of needle.

Next row (dec): Skip next row, pick up and knit 1 st in first st of next row of previous rnd, slide sts to opposite end of needle, k2tog, k1, skp—3 sts.

Work 1 row even but do not slide sts to opposite end of needle.

Next row (dec): Skip next row, pick up and knit 1 st in first st of next row of previous rnd, slide sts to opposite end of needle, k2tog, skp—2 sts.

Work 1 row even but do not slide sts to opposite end of needle.

Next row (dec): Skip next row, pick up and knit 1 st in first st of next row of previous rnd, slide sts to opposite end of needle, s2kp—1 st rem. Do not cut yarn.

RIBBING

Place rem st on cir needle. With RS facing, pick up and knit 103 sts evenly spaced along lower edge—104 sts. Pm, join for working in rnds.

Rnd 1: *K2, p2; rep from * around.

Rep rnd 1 six more times.

BO all sts in patt.

finishing

Weave in ends.

silver plates
DRAGON-SCALE CLOCHE

This dragon-scale beanie is a fairy-tale combination of alternating lace and cable panels knit from the bottom up in the round. A garter-stitch brim allows for stretch, while the lacework keeps it light and airy.

Designed by Robin Melanson

Finished Size

About 19½" (49.5 cm) circumference and 8¾" (22 cm) long along front.

Yarn

Worsted weight (#4 Medium).

Shown here: Cascade Yarns *Pacific* (40% superwash merino, 60% acrylic; 213 yd [195 m]/100 g): #24 platinum, 1 skein.

Needles

Size U.S. 7 (4.5 mm): 16" (40 cm) circular (cir) and 5 double-pointed (dpn).

Adjust needle size if necessary to obtain the correct gauge.

Notions

Stitch markers; cable needle (cn); tapestry needle.

Gauge

21 sts and 30 rnds = 4" (10 cm) over dragon-scale patt (see chart).

Note

There is no need to hide the wraps when completing the short-rows because the garter stitch naturally hides the wraps in the pattern.

Cloche

With cir needle, CO 102 sts. Place marker (pm), and join for working in rnd, being careful not to twist sts. Rnds beg at center back.

Work 7 rnds in garter st, ending with a purl rnd—4 ridges.

SHAPE EDGING

Short-row 1 (RS): Knit to last 10 sts, w&t.

Short-row 2 (WS): Knit to last 10 sts, w&t.

Short-row 3 (RS): Knit to 10 sts before last wrapped st, w&t.

Short-row 4 (WS): Knit to 10 sts before last wrapped st, w&t.

Next row (RS): Knit to end. Do not turn.

Next rnd: Purl to last 2 sts, sl 2 to RH needle, remove beg-of-rnd m, sl 2 sts back onto RH needle, pm for new beg of rnd.

Work chart rnds 1–12 three times; piece measures about 5" (12.5 cm) from top of garter st band.

SHAPE CROWN

Work chart rnds 13–21 once, dec as indicated and changing to dpns when there are too few sts to work comfortably on cir needle—42 sts.

Next rnd (dec): Sl 1, *k2tog, yo, k3tog, yo, k2tog; rep from * to last 6 sts, k2tog, yo, k3tog, yo, k2tog (last st of rnd with first st of previous rnd)—30 sts.

Next rnd (dec): (K2tog) to end—15 sts.

Cut yarn, leaving an 8" (20.5 cm) tail, thread tail through rem sts, pull tight to close hole, and fasten off on WS.

Finishing

Weave in ends. Block to finished measurements.

☐	knit
○	yo
╲	ssk
╱	k2tog
⃰	k3tog
⃰	sssk
▨	no stitch
⤬	2/2 LC (see Stitch Guide)
☐	pattern rep

Dragon-Scale Chart

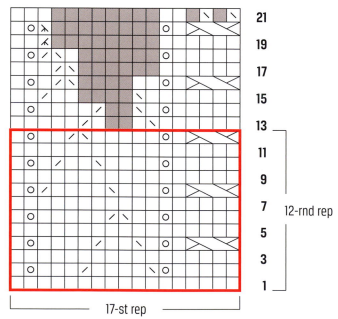

17-st rep

12-rnd rep

hers & his
CABLED-BRIM TAM AND BEANIE

Two heads (or hats) are better than one! The cabled band of both hats is worked first and bound off, then the ends are joined to create a brim. It's then flipped sideways and stitches are picked up along the edge and worked in stockinette stitch to create the body of the hat. Make one for your honey and one for yourself.

Designed by Hilary Smith Callis

Finished Sizes

Tam: 17 (19)" (43 [48.5] cm) circumference to fit head circumference up to 20 (23)" (51 [58.5] cm); 8¼ (9)" (21 [23] cm) high. Shown in size 17" (43 cm).

Beanie: 17 (19)" (43 [48.5] cm) circumference to fit head circumference up to 20 (23)" (51 [58.5] cm); 7¼ (8)" (18.5 [20.5] cm) high. Shown in size 19" (48.5 cm).

Left: "Hers" tam

Yarn

Worsted weight (#4 Medium).

Shown here: Cascade Yarns *Pacific* (40% superwash merino, 60% acrylic; 213 yd [195 m]/100 g): #10 olive, 1 skein for each hat or size.

Needles

Size U.S. 7 (4.5 mm): 16" (40 cm) circular (cir) and set of 4 double-pointed (dpn).

Adjust needle sizes if necessary to obtain the correct gauge.

Notions

Stitch marker; cable needle (cn); tapestry needle.

Gauge

18 sts and 23 rnds = 4" (10 cm) over St st.

Note

Instructions for both hats are given together, with the Beanie instructions in brackets [ ]. If only one set of instructions are given with no brackets, or unless otherwise specified, the instructions apply to both hats.

Tam and Beanie

BRIM

With cir needle or 2 dpns, CO 16 sts.

Row 1 and all other WS rows: P3, k2, p8, k2, p1.

Row 2 (RS): K1, p2, 2/2 RC, 2/2 LC, p2, k3.

Rows 4, 6, 10, and 12: K1, p2, k8, p2, k3.

Row 8: K1, p2, 2/2 LC, 2/2 RC, p2, k3.

Rep rows 1–12 six (seven) more times, then rep rows 1–10 once more; piece should measure 17 (19)" (43 [48.5] cm) from beg.

BO all sts in patt.

Cut yarn, leaving a tail 3 times the width of the cabled strip. Seam ends of strip tog, being careful not to twist.

With cir needle and RS facing, beg at seam and pick up and knit 94 (106) [81 (90)] sts along "k1" edge of cabled strip (beg of RS rows). Place marker (pm) for beg of rnd. Join to work in rnds.

TAM ONLY

Next rnd (inc): *K5 (7), M1; rep from * 13 (9) more times, **k6, M1; rep from ** 3 (5) more times—112 (122) sts.

Work even in St st until piece measures 6 (7)" (15 [18] cm) from bottom edge.

Next rnd (dec): Work in St st and dec 0 (2) sts evenly spaced—112 (120) sts.

BEANIE ONLY

Work even in St st until piece measures 5¼ (5¾)" (13.5 [14.5] cm) from bottom edge.

Next rnd (dec): Work in St st and dec 1 (2) st(s) evenly spaced—80 (88) sts.

SHAPE CROWN

Rnd 1: *K12 (13) [8, 9], k2tog; rep from * to end—8 sts dec'd.

Rnd 2: Knit.

Rnd 3: *K11 (12) [7, 8], k2tog; rep from * to end—8 sts dec'd.

Rnd 4: Knit.

Rnd 5: *K10 (11) [6, 7], k2tog; rep from * to end—8 sts dec'd.

Rnd 6: *K9 (10) [5, 6], k2tog; rep from * to end—8 sts dec'd.

Cont dec in this manner every rnd, with 1 fewer st between each k2tog every rnd 9 (10) [5, 6] more times—8 sts rem.

TAM ONLY

Next rnd (dec): (K2tog) 4 times—4 sts rem.

Cut yarn, leaving an 8" (20.5 cm) tail, thread tail through rem sts, pull tight to close hole, fasten off on WS.

Finishing

Weave in ends. Block hat to finished measurements.

Right: "His" beanie

hammer time
TEXTURED SLOUCH–HAT

A deep cabled-rib brim keeps this slouchy hat snugly in place. The allover hammer stitch creates interesting texture while allowing for a slouchier fit. Decreasing is camouflaged nicely in the crown ribbing pattern.

Designed by Faina Goberstein

Finished Sizes

17¼ (20¼)" (44 [51.5] cm) circumference at ribbed brim. Sample is made in size 20¼" (51.5 cm).

Yarn

Worsted weight (#4 Medium).

Shown here: Cascade Yarns *Pacific* (40% merino wool, 60% acrylic; 213 yd [195 m]/100 g): #32 country blue, 1 skein.

Needles

Hat: size U.S. 5 (3.75 mm): 16" (40 cm) circular (cir) and set of 5 double-pointed (dpn).

Brim: size U.S. 3 (3.25 mm): 16" (40 cm) circular (cir).

Adjust needle sizes if necessary to obtain the correct gauge.

Notions

Markers (m); cable needle (cn); tapestry needle.

Gauge

24 sts and 32 rnds = 4" (10 cm) over chart A on larger needles.

26 sts and 34 rnds = 4" (10 cm) over cabled rib on smaller needles.

Stitch Guide

1/1 LC (1 OVER 1 LEFT CROSS):
Sl next st onto cn and hold in front of work, k1, k1 from cn.

CABLED RIB (MULTIPLE OF 4 STS)

Rnd 1: *K2, p2; rep from * to end.

Rnd 2: *1/1 LC, p2; rep from * to end.

Rep rnds 1 and 2 for patt.

Hat

BRIM

With smaller cir needle and using long-tail cast-on, CO 112 (132) sts. Place marker (pm), and join for working in the rnd, being careful not to twist sts.

Work in cabled rib for 2" (5 cm), ending with rnd 1 of patt.

Next rnd (inc): Work 7 (11) sts in patt, M1; rep from * 15 (11) more times—128 (144) sts.

BODY

Change to larger cir needle. Work chart A (hammer st) until hat measures about 7" (18 cm) from beg, ending with rnd 2 of patt.

SHAPE CROWN

Note: Change to dpns when too few sts rem to work comfortably on cir needle.

Place markers after every 16 sts to keep track of decreases.

BEGIN CHART B

Next rnd (dec): Work rnd 1 of chart B 8 (9) times—120 (135) sts.

Work rnds 2–20 of chart B—16 (18) sts rem.

Cut yarn, leaving an 8" (20.5 cm) tail, thread tail through rem sts, pull tightly to close hole, fasten off on WS.

finishing

Weave in ends.

□	knit
•	purl
∕	k2tog
⸜	p2tog
▧	no stitch
▭	pattern rep

Chart A

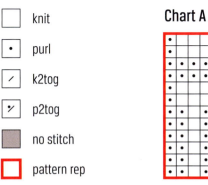

8-st rep

Chart B

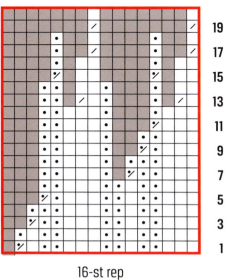

16-st rep

secret stash

FAIR ISLE HEADBAND

Much of the work in this beautiful headband is done post knitting. The band is knit in the round in a basic Fair Isle pattern, while the earflaps are duplicate stitched and embroidered with bullion stitch, then attached to the band and finished off with single crochet trim. The flaps create a secret pocket perfect for storing your bus or subway pass, lucky penny, or any tiny treasures.

Designed by Galina Carroll

Finished Size

Circumference 19" (48.5 cm).

Yarn

Worsted weight (#4 Medium).

Shown here: Cascade Yarns *Pacific* (40% superwash merino, 60% acrylic; 213 yd [195 m]/100 g): #37 clover (A), 1 skein; #52 geranium (B), 1 skein; #44 Italian plum (C), 1 skein; #36 Christmas red (D), 1 skein.

Needles

Size U.S. 7 (4.5 mm): 16" (40 cm) circular (cir).

Adjust needle size if necessary to obtain the correct gauge.

Notions

Size E/4 (3.5 mm) crochet hook; embroidery needle; 2 stitch holders; tapestry needle.

Gauge

19 sts and 20 rows = 4" (10 cm) over chart B.

Note

See Glossary for chain stitch, duplicate stitch, and bullion stitch.

Earflap (make 2)

With C, CO 11 sts. Do not join.

Rows 1-28: With A and C only, work chart A—17 sts. Place sts on holder.

Embroider earflaps foll chart (see Glossary).

Headband

With C, CO 26 sts, with WS of earflap facing, k17 sts from one holder, CO 30 sts, with WS of rem earflap facing, k17 sts from holder—90 sts.

Place marker (pm) and join for working in rnds.

Rnds 1-16: Work chart B.

BO pwise with C.

Finishing

With crochet hook and C, and RS of earflap facing, work sc along lowest edge and two adjoining edges. Fold earflap to RS along fold line (see chart), then cont sc around rem edges and fold edge; fasten off. Sew slanted edges of top part to the headband, leaving top edge open for a pocket.

Chart A

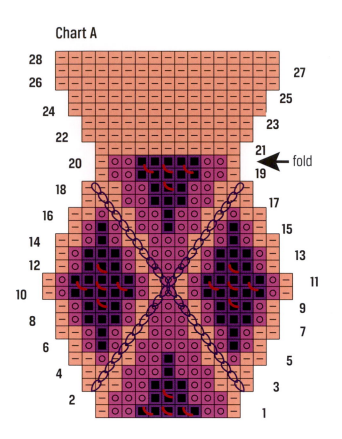

← fold

Chart B

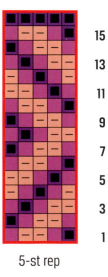

5-st rep

	with A, knit on RS; purl on WS
	with B, knit on RS; purl on WS
	with C, knit on RS; purl on WS
	pattern rep
	knit with B; duplicate st with A
	chain st with C
	bullion st with D

Warm & Wonderful Mittens

Raise your hand if you need a new pair of handwarmers! The designs in this chapter run the gamut from fingerless wristers that will keep your digits free (for more knitting) to snug mittens that will warm *your* mitts in the coldest weather.

chain gang
CABLED MITTENS

The meandering cable patterns running up the middle of each of these structured mittens are mirror images of each other. The garter-stitch background allows the cables to really pop.

Designed by Angela Hahn

Finished Size

11¾" (30 cm) long if measured along cable patt, 11" (28 cm) long if measured on palm side; 7½" (19 cm) hand circumference. Sized to fit most women.

Yarn

Worsted weight (#4 Medium).

Shown here: Cascade Yarns *Pacific* (40% superwash merino, 60% acrylic; 213 yd [195 m]/100 g): #38 violet, 1 skein.

Needles

Set of 4 size U.S. 7 (4.5 mm) double-pointed (dpn).

Adjust needle size if necessary to obtain the correct gauge.

Notions

Stitch markers; tapestry needle; 2 cable needles (cn).

Gauges

18½ sts and 37 rounds = 4" (10 cm) in garter stitch, unblocked.

33 rnds = 4" (10 cm) in cable patt, unblocked.

Note

To preserve the depth of texture in the cable and garter-stitch patterns, do not block these mittens when complete.

CABLE PATTERN (WORKED OVER 11 STS AND 12 RNDS)

Note that the cable cross is worked differently for each hand.

Rnds 1-11: P1, k9, p1.

Left mitten rnd 12: P1, sl next 6 sts to cn and hold in front of work, k3, sl last 3 sts from cn back to LH needle, pass cn with 3 rem sts to back of work, k3, k3 from cn, p1.

Right mitten rnd 12: P1, sl next 3 sts to first cn and hold in back of work, sl next 3 sts to second cn and hold in front of work, k3, k3 from second cn, k3 from first cn, p1.

Left Mitten

Using knitted cast-on, CO 38 sts. Distribute sts evenly among 3 dpn. Place marker (pm), and join for working in the rnd, being careful not to twist sts.

Rnd 1: Purl.

Rnd 2: Knit to last 11 sts, pm for start of cable panel, p1, k 9, p1.

Rnd 3: Rep rnd 1.

Rnd 4: Knit to last 11 sts, work rnd 1 of cable patt.

Rnd 5: Purl to last 11 sts, work rnd 2 of cable patt.

Rnds 6-48: Cont garter st and cable patt sections as established, ending on a knit rnd for garter st.

THUMB GUSSET

Rnd 49: Purl to 8 sts before cable panel, pm, p1 in rnd below, p1, p1 in rnd below, pm, work to end—2 sts inc'd.

Rnd 50: Work inc sts in garter st, work even in established patt.

Rnd 51 (gusset inc): Work in patt to gusset m, p1 in rnd below, work to next m, p1 in rnd below, work to end—2 sts inc'd.

Rnds 52-55: Rep last 2 rnds twice more—46 sts total; 9 sts between gusset markers.

Rnds 56-60: Work even in patt.

Rnd 61: Work in patt to gusset m, place 9 gusset sts on holder for thumb, remove gusset m, turn, using knitted cast-on to CO 6 sts over gap, turn, join to rem sts and work to end—43 sts.

Rnds 62-91: Working CO sts in garter st, work in patt as established.

Rnd 92: K6, pm, k20, pm, k6, work to end.

SHAPE TOP

Rnd 1 (dec): *Purl to 3 sts before m, p2tog, p2, p2tog; rep from * once more, work to end—4 sts dec'd.

Rnd 2: Work even in patt.

Rep rnds 1 and 2 twice more—8 sts dec'd.

Rnd 3 (dec): P2tog, p2, p2tog, purl to 3 sts before next m, p2tog, p2, p2tog, p1, sl next 6 sts to cn and hold in front of work, k3tog, sl last 3 sts from cn back to LH needle, pass cn with 3 rem sts to back of work, k3, then (ssk, k1) from cn, p1—24 sts rem. Knit first 2 sts of next rnd. Cut yarn, leaving an 18" (45.5 cm) tail for three-needle BO.

Turn work inside out. Place next 12 sts on 1 dpn; place rem 12 sts on 2nd dpn. Using 3rd dpn, BO all sts using 3-needle BO.

Right Mitten

Using knitted cast-on, CO 38 sts. Distribute sts evenly among 3 dpn. Pm, and join for working in the rnd, being careful not to twist sts.

Rnds 1-48: Work as for left mitten, working cable patt over last 11 sts, and right mitten rnd 12.

THUMB GUSSET

Rnd 49: P7, pm, p1 in rnd below, p1, p1 in rnd below, pm, work in patt to end—2 sts inc'd.

Rnds 50-98: Work as for left mitten, working right mitten rnd 12 of cable patt—31 sts rem.

Rnd 99: P2tog, p2, p2tog, purl to 3 sts before next m, p2tog, p2, p2tog, p1, sl next 3 sts to first cn and hold in back of work, sl next 3 sts to second cn and hold in front of work, k2tog, (k1, k3) from second cn, sssk from first cn, p1—24 sts rem. Knit first 2 sts of next yarn. Cut yarn, leaving an 18" (45.5 cm) tail for three-needle BO. Using three-needle BO, join sts at top of mitten as for left mitten.

Thumb (worked same for both hands)

With RS facing and using dpn, pick up and knit 8 sts along CO edge. Place 9 held sts on 2 dpn—17 sts. Pm and join for working in the rnd. Beg rnds over held sts.

Next rnd (dec): P9, p2tog, p4, p2tog—15 sts.

Next rnd: Knit.

Next rnd: Purl.

Rep last 2 rnds 7 more times.

Next rnd (dec): *K1, k2tog; rep from * to end of rnd—10 sts.

Next rnd (dec): P2tog to end of rnd—5 sts. Cut yarn, leaving an 8" (20.5 cm) tail, thread tail through rem sts, pull tight to close hole, fasten off on WS.

Finishing

Weave in ends, closing any holes along base of thumb.

turquoise trail
FAIR ISLE WRISTERS

The bright Fair Isle pattern of these striking wristers pays homage to the colors of the Southwestern United States. They'll surely keep your hands warm during cool evenings in the desert.

Designed by Sauniell Connally

Finished Size

One size fits most.

6½" (16.5 cm) hand circumference and 6¼" (16 cm) long.

Yarn

Worsted weight (#4 Medium).

Shown here: Cascade Yarns *Pacific* (40% superwash merino, 60% acrylic; 213 yd [195 m]/100 g): #51 honeysuckle pink (A), 1 skein; #40 peacock (B), 1 skein; #13 gold (C), 1 skein; #57 Dijon (D), 1 skein.

Needles

Size U.S. 6 (4 mm): 24" or 32" (60 or 80 cm) circular (cir).

Size U.S. 7 (4.5 mm): 24" or 32" (60 or 80 cm) circular (cir).

Adjust needle sizes if necessary to obtain the correct gauge.

Notions

2 stitch markers; waste yarn; tapestry needle.

Gauges

26 sts and 30 rows = 4" (10 cm) over colorwork pattern, using larger needles.

Note

Instructions are based on the one-circular magic-loop method. If using two short circular needles or double-pointed needles, please adjust accordingly.

Wrister (make 2)

With smaller needle and A, CO 36 sts. Divide sts evenly on needle to work magic-loop method (see Glossary). Place marker (pm), and join for working in rnds, being careful not to twist sts.

Rnd 1: *K2, p2; rep from * to end.

Rep last rnd 5 more times.

Change to larger needle.

Next rnd (inc): With D, *k9, m1, k9, pm; rep from * once more—2 sts inc'd.

Knit 1 rnd even.

With A, knit 2 rnds.

Next rnd (inc): With D, *k1, m1, k17, m1, k1, sm; rep from * to end—42 sts.

Rnds 1–15: Work foll color chart.

Rnd 16 (thumb placement): Work 3 sts in established patt, with waste yarn k6, slip these 6 sts back onto LH needle, cont in patt to end.

Rnds 17–29: Work foll color chart.

Next rnd (dec): With A, *k2tog, k19, sm; rep from * to end—40 sts rem.

Change to smaller needle.

Next rnd: With D, knit.

Next rnd: *K1, p1; rep from * to end.

Next rnd: With A, cont rib patt.

Rep last rnd 4 more times.

BO all sts in patt.

THUMB

Remove waste yarn, exposing 12 loops and place exposed loops on smaller needle with 6 sts along top of opening on one end and 6 sts along bottom of opening on opposite end.

Next rnd: With A, pick up and knit 1 st in gap at one end of opening, k6 from one needle, pick up and knit 1 st in gap at opposite end of opening, knit rem 6 sts—14 sts. Pm for beg of rnd, and join for working in rnds.

Rnd 1: *K1, p1; rep from * to end.

Rep last rnd 4 more times.

BO all sts in patt.

finishing

Weave in ends. Block to finished measurements.

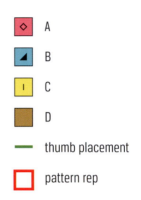

◇	A
◢	B
I	C
	D
—	thumb placement
▢	pattern rep

Color Chart

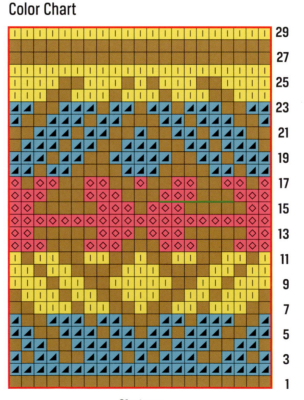

21-st rep

fisherman's friend
TEXTURED-CUFF GAUNTLETS

With handsome ribbing around the cuffs, these gauntlets naturally hug the wearer's wrist for a warm fit. Once you're past the ribbing, it's smooth sailing through the stockinette-stitch body of the mittens.

Designed by Debbie O' Neill

Finished Sizes

About 7¼ (8¾, 10)" (18.5 [22, 25.5] cm) hand circumference. Shown in size 7¼" (18.5 cm).

Yarn

Worsted weight (#4 Medium).

Shown here: Cascade Yarns *Pacific* (40% superwash merino, 60% acrylic; 213 yd [195 m]/100 g): #55 lichen, 1 (1, 2) skein(s).

Needles

Set of 4 size U.S. 4 (3.5 mm) double-pointed (dpn).

Adjust needle size if necessary to obtain the correct gauge.

Notions

Scrap yarn; stitch markers; tapestry needle.

Gauge

25 sts and 34 rows = 4" (10 cm) over St st.

GANSEY RIBBING (MULTIPLE OF 4 STS)

Rnds 1 and 2: *K2, p2; rep from * to end of rnd.

Rnds 3 and 4: *P2, k2; rep from * to end of rnd.

Rnds 5, 6, 9, and 10: Rep rnd 1.

Rnds 7 and 8: Rep rnd 2.

Rnds 11, 13, and 15: Knit.

Rnds 12, 14, and 16: Purl.

Rnds 17-26: Rep rnd 1.

Rnds 27, 29, and 31: Knit.

Rnds 28, 30, and 32: Purl.

Gauntlets

CUFF

CO 44 (52, 60) sts. Divide sts on dpn as foll: 14 (18, 20) sts on needle 1; 16 (16, 20) sts on needle 2; and 14 (18, 20) sts on needle 3. Place marker (pm), and join for working in the rnd, being careful not to twist sts. Work rnds 1–32 of the gansey ribbing.

HAND

Cont in St st for 5 (7, 9) rnds.

LEFT THUMB GUSSET

Next rnd (inc): K8 (12, 16), pm, M1, k1, M1, pm, knit to end of rnd—2 sts inc'd.

Next rnd: Knit.

Next rnd (inc): K8 (12, 16), sm, M1, knit to m, M1, sm, knit to end of rnd—2 sts inc'd.

Next rnd: Knit.

Rep last 2 rnds 5 (6, 7) more times—58 (68, 78) sts total; 15 (17, 19) sts between gusset markers.

Next rnd: K8, sl 15 (17, 19) sts between m onto scrap yarn for thumb, CO 3 sts over gap, then knit to end of rnd—46 (54, 62) sts.

RIGHT THUMB GUSSET

Next rnd (inc): Knit to last 9 (13, 17) sts, pm, M1, k1, M1, knit to end of rnd—2 sts inc'd.

Next rnd: Knit.

Next rnd (inc): Knit to m, sm, M1, knit to m, M1, sm, knit to end of rnd—2 sts inc'd.

Next rnd: Knit.

Rep last 2 rnds 5 (6, 7) more times—58 (68, 78) sts total; 15 (17, 19) sts between gusset markers.

Next rnd: Knit to m, sl 15 (17, 19) sts between m onto scrap yarn for thumb, CO 3 sts over gap, then knit to end of rnd—46 (54, 62) sts.

BOTH HANDS

Cont even in St st until mitten measures about 1¼ (1½, 1¾)" (3.2 [3.8, 4.5] cm) less than desired hand length.

SHAPE TOP

Setup rnd: K11 (13, 15), pm, k23 (27, 31), pm, knit to end of rnd.

Next rnd (dec): Knit to 3 sts before m, k2tog, k1, sm, k1, ssk, knit to 3 sts before m, k2tog, k1, sm, k1, ssk, knit to end of rnd—4 sts dec'd.

Next rnd: Knit.

Rep last 2 rnds 5 (6, 7) more times—22 (26, 30) sts rem. Knit to m, rearrange sts with palm sts on 1 dpn and back of hand sts on 2nd dpn. Graft the top of the mitten closed using Kitchener stitch (see Glossary).

THUMB

Return held 15 (17, 19) thumb sts to dpn as foll: 5 (6, 6) sts on needle 1; 5 (6, 7) sts on needle 2; and 5 (5, 6) sts on needle 3. Pick up and knit 1 st in gap between hand and top of opening, 3 sts in CO sts above gap, then 1 st in gap between hand and top of opening—20 (22, 24) sts. Pm for beg of rnd and join for working in the rnd. Cont even in St st for 5 rnds.

Next rnd (dec): K15 (17, 19), ssk, k1, k2tog—18 (20, 22) sts rem. Work even until length is about ¼" (6 mm) shorter than the desired thumb length.

SHAPE TOP

Next rnd (dec): K0 (1, 0), *k1, k2tog; rep from *, ending k0 (1, 1)—12 (14, 15) sts rem.

Next rnd: Knit.

Next rnd (dec): *K2tog; rep from *, ending k0 (0, 1)—6 (7, 8) sts rem.

Cut yarn, leaving an 8" (20.5 cm) tail, thread through rem sts, pull tight to close hole, fasten off on WS.

Finishing

Weave in ends. Wash and block if desired.

green gables
CABLED GAUNTLETS

These textured unisex gauntlets feature an easy eight-stitch cable pattern worked in the round.
Quick to knit and perfectly portable, they're the ideal pattern for the on-the-go knitter.

Designed by Lynn Wilson

Finished Size

About 6½" (16.5 cm) hand circumference and 10¾" (27.5 cm) long.

Yarn

Worsted weight (#4 Medium).

Shown here: Cascade Yarns *Pacific* (40% superwash merino, 60% acrylic; 213 yd [195 m]/100 g): #56 Kelly green, 1 skein.

Needles

U.S. size 6 (4 mm): set of 4 or 5 double-pointed (dpn).

Adjust needle size if necessary to obtain the correct gauge.

Notions

Stitch marker; cable needle (cn); size F/5 (3.75 mm) crochet hook.

Gauges

21 sts and 25 rows = 4" (10 cm) over St st.

Gauntlet (make 2)

CO 48 sts. Divide sts evenly over 3 or 4 dpns. Place marker (pm), and join for working in rnd, being careful not to twist sts.

Work rnds 1–8 of zigzag cable patt 5 times, or to desired length. (**Note:** To make gauntlets shorter, work 3 or 4 reps of patt; to make gauntlets longer, work 5 or more reps of patt. Remember to adjust yarn requirements accordingly.)

THUMB OPENING

Next rnd (inc): *K1, p2, k3, p2; rep from * to end, M1—49 sts.

Divide work and beg working back and forth as foll:

Row 1 and all other WS rows: *P1, k2, p3, k2; rep from * to last st, p1.

Row 2 (RS): *K1, p2, 1/2 LC, p2; rep from * to last st, k1.

Row 4: *K1, p2, k3, p2; rep from * to last st, k1.

Row 6: *K1, p2, 1/2 RC, p2; rep from * to last st, k1.

Rows 7–14: Rep rows 1–6 once, then rep rows 1 and 2 once more. Do not turn work at end of last row.

Rejoin to work in rnds again. Pm for beg of rnd.

Next rnd (dec): *K1, p2, k3, p2; rep from *, ending last rep p1, p2tog—48 sts.

HAND

Cont from rnd 3 of zigzag cable patt and work 13 more rnds, ending with rnd 7.

Next rnd (dec): *K1, p2, k1, k2tog, p2; rep from * to end—42 sts.

BO all sts in patt.

Finishing

With crochet hook, work 1 rnd of sc around thumb opening.

Weave in ends. Block to finished measurements if desired.

handiwork

TEXTURED FINGERLESS MITTS

These mitts are the perfect quick knit for gift giving. Knit in the round in seed stitch, with ribbing on the top and bottom and a sophisticated color palette, the unisex design is sure to please all.

Designed by Sauniell Connally

Finished Size

One size fits most.

7" (18 cm) hand circumference and 6½" (16.5 cm) long.

Yarn

Worsted weight (#4 Medium).

Shown here: Cascade Yarns *Pacific* (40% superwash merino, 60% acrylic; 213 yd [195 m]/100 g): #9 sand (A), 1 skein; #25 burnt orange (B), 1 skein; #28 blue (C), 1 skein.

Needles

Size U.S. 6 (4 mm): 24" or 32" (60 or 80 cm) circular (cir).

Size U.S. 7 (4.5 mm): 24" or 32" (60 or 80 cm) circular (cir).

Adjust needle sizes if necessary to obtain the correct gauge.

Notions

2 stitch markers; waste yarn; tapestry needle.

Gauge

22½ sts and 32 rows = 4" (10 cm) over simple seed st patt, using larger needles.

Note

Instructions are based on the one-circular magic-loop method. If using two short circular needles or double-pointed needles, please adjust accordingly.

Stitch Guide

SIMPLE SEED STITCH (MULTIPLE OF 4 STS)

Rnd 1: *K1, p1, k2; rep from * to end.

Rnd 2: Knit.

Rnd 3: *K2, p1, k1; rep from* to end.

Rnd 4: Knit.

Rep rnds 1–4 for simple seed st patt.

mitts (make 2)

With smaller needle and A, CO 36 sts. Divide sts evenly on needle to work magic-loop method (see Glossary). Place marker (pm), and join for working in rnds, being careful not to twist sts.

Rnd 1: *K2, p2; rep from * to end.

Rep last rnd 5 more times.

Change to larger needle.

Work 5 rnds in simple seed st.

Next rnd (inc): Working next row of patt, *k1, m1, k16, m1, k1; rep from * to end—40 sts.

Cont even in patt for 15 rnds.

Next rnd (thumb opening): Work 3 sts in established patt, with waste yarn k6, slip these 6 sts back onto LH needle, cont in patt to end.

Cont even in patt for 9 rnds.

Next rnd: K39, sl 1.

Next rnd: With B, work in established patt.

Next rnd: K39, sl 1.

Next rnd: Work 1 rnd even.

Next rnd: With A, knit.

Next rnd: Work 39 sts, sl 1.

With C, work 2 rnds in established patt.

Change to smaller needle.

Next rnd: *K2, p2*; rep from * to end.

Rep last rnd for 5 rnds.

BO all sts in patt.

THUMB

Remove waste yarn and place 12 exposed loops on smaller needle with 6 sts along top of opening on one end and 6 sts along bottom of opening on opposite end.

Next rnd: With A, pick up and knit 1 st in gap at one end of opening, k6 from one needle, pick up and knit 1 st in gap at opposite end of opening, knit rem 6 sts—14 sts. Pm for beg of rnd and join for working in rnds.

Rnd 1: *K1, p1; rep from * to end.

Rep last rnd 4 more times. BO all sts in patt.

finishing

Weave in ends. Block to finished measurements.

lattice work
CABLED MITTS

Cabled cuffs branch into a lattice cable pattern on back of the hand of these snug mittens. The patterns are different for each hand, making these mitts a cable lover's dream.

Designed by Debbie O'Neill

Finished Sizes

About 6¼ (7, 8¼)" (16 [18, 21] cm) hand circumference. Shown in size 6¼" (16 cm).

Yarn

Worsted weight (#4 Medium).

Shown here: Cascade Yarns *Pacific* (40% superwash merino, 60% acrylic; 213 yd [195 m]/100 g): #39 French blue, 1 (1, 2) skein(s).

Needles

Set of 4 size U.S. 4 (3.5 mm) double-pointed (dpn).

Adjust needle size if necessary to obtain the correct gauge.

Notions

Cable needle (cn); scrap yarn; stitch markers; tapestry needle.

Gauge

24 sts and 34 rows = 4" (10 cm) over St st.

Notes

The cables will cause the mittens to appear very narrow. However, they will stretch nicely to fit the hand snugly.

The hand of the mitten is arranged such that the lattice pattern runs up the back of the hand. The remaining stitches (palm and sides of the hand) are worked in St st. The stitches are arranged on the needles such that the end of the round is at about the middle of the palm.

2/2 RC (2 over 2 right cross):
Sl next 2 sts onto cn and hold in back of work, k2, k2 from cn.

2/2 LC (2 over 2 left cross):
Sl next 2 sts onto cn and hold in front of work, k2, k2 from cn.

2/1 LPC (2 over 1 left purl cross):
Sl next 2 sts onto cn and hold in front of work, p1, k2 from cn.

2/1 RPC (2 over 1 left purl cross):
Sl next st onto cn and hold in back of work, k2, p1 from cn.

2/4 LC (2 over 4 left cross):
Sl next 2 sts onto cn and hold in front of work, p2, k2 from LH needle, then k2 from cn.

2/4 RC (2 over 4 right cross):
Sl next 4 sts onto cn and hold in back of work, k2 from LH needle, then (p2, k2) from cn.

CABLE RIBBING (LEFT HAND; MULTIPLE OF 8 STS)

Rnds 1–6: *K2, p2; rep from * to end of rnd.

Rnd 7: *2/1 LPC, 2/1 RPC, p2; rep from * to end of rnd.

Rnd 8: *P1, k4, p3; rep from * to end of rnd.

Rnd 9: *P1, 2/2 LC, p3; rep from * to end of rnd.

Rnds 10–12: Rep rnd 8.

Rnd 13: Rep rnd 9.

Rnd 14: Rep rnd 8.

Rnd 15: *2/1 RPC, 2/1 LPC, p2; rep from * to end of rnd.

Rnds 16–21: *K2, p2; rep from * to end of rnd.

CABLE RIBBING (RIGHT HAND; MULTIPLE OF 8 STS)

Rnds 1–6: *K2, p2; rep from * to end of rnd.

Rnd 7: *2/1 LPC, 2/1 RPC, p2; rep from * to end of rnd.

Rnd 8: *P1, k4, p3; rep from * to end of rnd.

Rnd 9: *P1, 2/2 RC, p3; rep from * to end of rnd.

Rnds 10–12: Rep rnd 8.

Rnd 13: Rept rnd 9.

Rnd 14: Rep rnd 8.

Rnd 15: *2/1 RPC, 2/1 LPC, p2; rep from * to end of rnd.

Rnds 16–21: *K2, p2; rep from * to end of rnd.

LATTICE PATTERN (LEFT HAND; PANEL OF 26 [30, 34] STS)

Rnds 1, 3, 5, 9, 11, and 13: K0 (2, 0), *k2, p2; rep from * to last 2 (4, 2) sts, end k2 (4, 2).

Rnd 2 and all even rnds: K0 (2, 0), *k2, p2; rep from * to last 2 (4, 2) sts, end k2 (4, 2).

Rnd 7: K0 (2, 0), *2/4 RC, p2; rep from * to last 2 (4, 2) sts, end k2 (4, 2).

Rnd 15: K2 (4, 2), *p2, 2/4 RC; rep from * to last 0 (2, 0) sts, end k0 (2, 0).

Rep rows 1–16 for patt.

LATTICE PATTERN (RIGHT HAND; PANEL OF 26 [30, 34] STS)

Rnds 1, 3, 5, 9, 11, and 13: K0 (2, 0), *k2, p2; rep from * to last 2 (4, 2) sts, end k2 (4, 2).

Rnd 2 and all even rnds: K0 (2, 0), *k2, p2; rep from * to last 2 (4, 2) sts, end k2 (4, 2).

Rnd 7: K0 (2, 0), *2/4 LC, p2; rep from * to last 2 (4, 2) sts, end k2 (4, 2).

Rnd 15: K2 (4, 2), *p2, 2/4 LC; rep from * to last 0 (2, 0) sts, end k0 (2, 0).

Rep rnds 1–16 for patt.

Left Mitten

CO 48 (56, 64) sts. Divide sts over 3 dpn as foll: 16 (16, 24) sts on needle 1; 16 (24, 16) sts on needle 2; and 16 (16, 24) sts on needle 3. Place marker (pm), and join for working in rnds, being careful not to twist sts. Work rnds 1–21 of the cable ribbing for left hand.

Setup rnd: K12 (14, 20), work lattice patt for left hand over next 26 (30, 34) sts, knit to end of rnd. Cont as established for 4 (6, 8) more rnds.

THUMB GUSSET

Next rnd (inc): K9 (11, 17), pm, M1, k1, M1, pm, work as established to end of rnd—2 sts inc'd.

Next rnd: Work in established patt.

Next rnd (inc): Knit to gusset m, sm, M1, knit to gusset m, M1, sm, work as established to end of rnd—2 sts inc'd.

Next rnd: Work in established patt.

Rep last 2 rnds 6 (7, 8) more times—64 (74, 84) sts total; 17 (19, 21) sts between gusset markers.

Next rnd: Knit to gusset m, sl 17 (19, 21) sts between gusset markers to scrap yarn for thumb, CO 3 sts over gap, then knit to end of rnd—50 (58, 66) sts.

Right Mitten

CO 48 (56, 64) sts. Divide sts over 3 dpn as foll: 16 (16, 24) sts on needle 1; 16 (24, 16) sts on needle 2; and 16 (16, 24) sts on needle 3. Pm for beg of rnd, and join for working in rnds, being careful not to twist sts. Work rnds 1–21 of the cable ribbing for right hand.

Setup rnd: K12 (14, 20), work lattice patt for right hand over next 26 (30, 34) sts, knit to end of rnd. Cont as established for 4 (6, 8) more rnds.

THUMB GUSSET

Next rnd (inc): Work as established to last 8 (10, 16) sts, pm, M1, k1, M1, pm, knit to end of rnd—2 sts inc'd.

Next rnd: Work in established patt.

Next rnd (inc): Work as established to gusset m, sm, M1, knit to gusset m, M1, sm, knit to end of rnd—2 sts inc'd.

Next rnd: Work in established patt.

Rep last 2 rnds 6 (7, 8) more times—64 (74, 84) sts total; 17 (19, 21) sts between gusset markers.

Next rnd: Knit to gusset m, sl 17 (19, 21) sts between gusset m to scrap yarn for thumb, CO 3 sts over gap, then knit to end of rnd—50 (58, 66) sts.

Both Mittens

Work even until mitten measures about 1½ (1¾, 2)" (4 [4.5, 5] cm) less than desired hand length.

Setup rnd: K12 (14, 20), pm, k1, ssk, work 20 (24, 28) sts in established pattern, k2tog, k1, pm, knit to end of rnd—48 (56, 64) sts rem. Work 1 rnd even.

Next rnd (dec): Knit to 3 sts before m, k2tog, k1, sm, k1, ssk, work to 3 sts before m, k2tog, k1, sm, k1, ssk, knit to end of rnd—4 sts dec'd. Work 1 rnd even.

Rep last 2 rnds 5 (6, 7) more times—24 (28, 32) sts rem. Knit to m, rearrange sts with palm sts on 1 dpn, and back of hand sts on 2nd dpn. Graft the top of the mitten closed using the Kitchener stitch (see Glossary).

THUMB

Place held 17 (19, 21) thumb sts on dpn as foll: 6 (6, 7) sts on needle 1; 6 (7, 7) sts on needle 2; and 5 (6, 7) sts on needle 3. Pick up and knit 5 sts onto needle 3—22 (24, 26) sts total. Pm and join for working in rnds, being careful not to twist sts.

Knit 5 rnds even.

Next rnd (dec): K17 (19, 21), ssk, k1, k2tog—20 (22, 24) sts rem. Work 1 rnd even.

Next rnd (dec): K17 (19, 21), sl 1, k2tog, psso—18 (20, 22) sts rem.

Work even until thumb is about ¼" (6 mm) shorter than desired length.

SHAPE TOP

Next rnd (dec): K0 (1, 0), *k1, k2tog; rep from *, ending k0 (1, 1)—12 (14, 15) sts rem.

Next rnd: Knit.

Next rnd (dec): *K2tog; rep from *, ending k0 (0, 1)—6 (7, 8) sts rem.

Cut yarn, leaving an 8" (20.5 cm) tail, thread tail through the rem sts, pull tight to close hole, fasten off on WS.

Finishing

Weave in ends. Wash and block if desired.

scandinavian inspiration

FAIR ISLE FINGERLESS MITTS

These unisex Fair Isle fingerless mitts will keep you cozy through autumn, winter, and into spring. Worked in the round with a thumb that's knit last, this is an ideal project for a beginning Fair Isle knitter. Switch up the colors to suit the wearer and make a pair for the whole family!

Designed by Mary Jane Mucklestone

Finished Size

8¼" (21 cm) hand circumference and 8¼" (21 cm) long.

Yarn

Worsted weight (#4 Medium).

Shown here: Cascade Yarns *Pacific* (40% superwash merino, 60% acrylic; 213 yd [195 m]/100 g): #1 cream (A), 1 skein; #39 French blue (B), 1 skein; #43 ruby (C), 1 skein; #33 cactus (D), 1 skein.

Needles

Size U.S. 3 (3.25 mm): set of 4 double-pointed (dpn).

Size U.S. 5 (3.75 mm): set of 4 double-pointed (dpn).

Adjust needle sizes if necessary to obtain the correct gauge.

Notions

Tapestry needle; 12" (30.5 cm) piece of smooth waste yarn.

Gauge

23 sts and 27 rnds = 4" (10 cm) over colorwork pattern, using larger needles.

Mitt (make 2)

With smaller dpn and A, CO 42 sts. Distribute sts evenly onto 3 dpn. Place marker (pm), and join for working in rnd, being careful not to twist sts.

Rnd 1: *K1, p1; rep from * to end.

Rep rnd 1 until rib measures 3" (7.5 cm).

Next rnd (inc): *Work 7 sts, M1; rep from * around—48 sts.

Change to larger dpn.

Next rnd: Knit.

Rnds 1–17: Work foll color chart.

Rnd 18 (thumb placement): K8 with waste yarn, slip these 8 sts back onto LH needle, work in chart to end.

Rnds 19–27: Work foll color chart.

Next rnd: With A, knit.

Next rnd (dec): *K6, k2tog; rep from * to end—42 sts.

Change to smaller dpn. Work in k1, p1 rib for ¾" (2 cm).

BO all sts in rib.

THUMB

With first smaller dpn and A, pick up and knit 8 sts in sts below waste yarn, with second smaller dpn pick up and knit 8 sts in sts above waste yarn—16 sts. Carefully remove waste yarn. Divide sts on lower needle evenly over 2 dpn (needles 1 and 2), leaving 8 sts on upper dpn on one needle (needle 3).

Rnd 1: Knit across sts of needle 1 and 2, pick up and k1 in corner of opening and place on needle 2, knit across sts on needle 3, pick up and k1 in corner of opening and place on needle 3—18 sts; 4 sts on needle 1, 5 sts on needle 2, and 9 sts on needle 3. Pm for beg of rnd and join for working in rnd.

Rnds 2 and 3: Knit.

Rnds 4–7: Work in k1, p1 rib.

BO all sts in rib.

Finishing

Weave in ends, taking care in the corners to close up any holes where the thumb joins the hand. Block to finished measurements, shaping mitts into right hand and left hand.

Color Chart

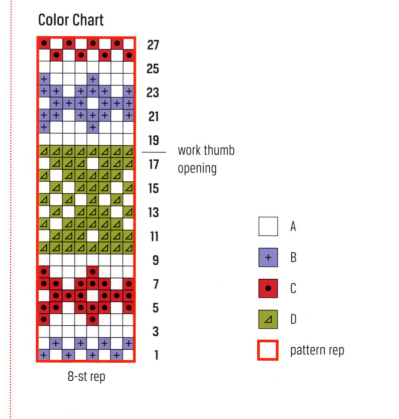

8-st rep

27
25
23
21
19 — work thumb opening
17
15
13
11
9
7
5
3
1

☐ A

+ B

● C

◿ D

▭ pattern rep

Cuddly Cowls & Scarves

We have your neck covered with gorgeous wraps, from feminine lace cowls and eye-catching colorwork gaiters to jaunty cabled mufflers and bold brioche scarves. If you're ready to take your garter-stitch scarves to the next level, this is the place to start.

brioche du jour
RIBBED SCARF

Knit in a high-contrast palette to make the ribbing pop, this interesting take on a classic brioche-stitch scarf goes modern with staggered color design. Knit it in your team colors to show your spirit (and keep you warm on the bleachers).

Designed by Nancy Marchant

Finished Size

7" (18 cm) wide and 64" (162.5 cm) long.

Yarn

Chunky weight (#5 Bulky).

Shown here: Cascade Yarns *Pacific Chunky* (40% superwash merino, 60% acrylic; 120 yd [110 m]/100 g): #25 burnt orange (light color/LC), 2 skeins; #45 concord grape (dark color/DC), 2 skeins.

Needles

Size U.S. 7 (4.5 mm): 16" (40 cm) circular (cir).

Adjust needle size if necessary to obtain the correct gauge.

Gauge

12 sts and 34 rows = 4" (10 cm) over two-color brioche.

Note

This stitch pattern uses a technique known as syncopated brioche. Syncopated brioche creates a motif by switching a knit column to a purled column and a purled column to a knit column. Because the knit columns protrude to the front and the purled columns recede, when syncopating using two colors, the light color (LC) will recede where it used to protrude and the dark color (DC) will protrude where it used to recede. This switch occurs every 20 rows until every stitch has been reversed.

Brioche Knitting Tips

Brioche knitting creates a cushy reversible ribbed fabric by working one stitch and slipping the next. Instead of carrying the working yarn in front or in back of the slipped stitch, bring the yarn over the stitch in the same way as working a yarnover; the yarnover will sit over the slipped stitch. The yarnover and the stitch it sits over are counted as one stitch, and both will be either knit or purled together with the stitch that it sits over on the following row.

By using two different colors and working in plain two-color brioche stitch, you will have straight vertical knitted columns of one color and purled columns of the second color. When the work is turned, the colors are reversed, and the knitted columns are in the second color and purled columns in the first.

Two rows are worked for each row that appears on the face of the fabric. Row 1A (light side, light color) is followed by Row 1B (light side, dark color). Both rows are considered Row 1. Row 2 consists of 2A (dark side, light color) and 2B (dark side, dark color).

In brioche color knitting, the yarnover of the row just worked is the last color that is used. So if you had to set down your knitting and are unsure which color you used last, look at the yarnovers.

The slip 1, yarnover (sl1yo) is always worked with the yarn in the front of the work before slipping the stitch. On a knit row, bring the yarn between needles to the front before slipping the stitch, then over the slipped stitch to the back of the work after slipping the stitch to have the yarn in place to knit the next stitch. On a purl row, the yarn is already at the front of the work, so slip the next stitch, then bring the yarn over the slipped stitch to the back of the work, then between the needles to the front again to purl the next stitch.

If you need to rip out some of your work, remove the needle and ravel to the point where you need to make the correction. Pick up the stitches with a smaller circular needle; this makes the stitches easier to pick up, then use the original needle to begin working again.

Stitch Guide

Sl1yo (slip 1, yarnover): With yarn in front of work, slip 1 purl-wise and bring yarn over needle to back of work; if the following stitch is a purl stitch, bring yarn between needles to front.

Scarf

CO 24 sts using the two-color Italian CO method (see Glossary), beginning with a knit st in LC.

Setup Row A: With LC, sl 1 wyb, *p1, sl1yo; rep from * to last st, p1. Do not turn work; slide sts to beg of row again.

Setup Row B: With DC, k1, *sl1yo, knit 1 st tog with the yo above it; rep from * to last st, drop DC to back of work, sl last st. Turn.

Row 1A: With LC, k1, *sl1yo, knit 1 st tog with the yo above it; rep from * to last st, drop LC to back of work, sl last st. Do not turn work; slide sts to beg of row again.

Row 1B: With DC, sl 1 wyb, *purl 1 st tog with the yo above it, sl1yo; rep from * to last st, p1. Turn.

Row 2A: With LC, sl 1 wyf, *purl 1 st tog with the yo above it, sl1yo; rep from * to last st, p1. Do not turn work; slide sts to beg of row again.

Row 2B: With DC, k1, *sl1yo, knit 1 st tog with the yo above it; rep from * to last st, drop DC to back of work, sl last st. Turn.

Rep rows 1A–2B nine more times.

Row 21A: With LC, k1, *sl1yo, knit 1 st tog with the yo above it; rep from * to last 3 sts, sl1yo, purl 1 st tog with the yo above it, drop LC to front of work, sl last st. Do not turn work; slide sts to beg of row again.

Row 21B: With DC, sl 1 wyf, *purl 1 st tog with the yo above it, sl1yo; rep from * to last st, k1. Turn.

Row 22A: With LC, sl 1 wyb, knit 1 st tog with the yo above it, sl1yo, *purl 1 st tog with the yo above it, sl1yo; rep from * to last st, p1. Do not turn work; slide sts to beg of row again.

Row 22B: With DC, p1, *sl1yo, knit 1 st tog with the yo above it; rep from * to last st, drop DC to back of work, sl last st. Turn.

Rep rows 21A–22B nine more times.

Row 41A: With LC, k1, *sl1yo, knit 1 st tog with the yo above it; rep from * to last 5 sts, (sl1yo, purl 1 st tog with the yo above it) twice, drop LC to front of work, sl last st. Do not turn work; slide sts to beg of row again.

Row 41B: With DC, sl 1 wyf, *purl 1 st tog with the yo above it, sl1yo; rep from * to last 3 sts, knit 1 st tog with the yo above it, sl1yo, k1. Turn.

Row 42A: With LC, sl 1 wyb, (knit 1 st tog with the yo above it, sl1yo) twice, *purl 1 st tog with the yo above it, sl1yo; rep from * to last st, p1. Do not turn work, slide sts to beg of row again.

Row 42B: P1, sl1yo, purl 1 st tog with the yo above it, *sl1yo, knit 1 st tog with the yo above it; rep from * to last st, drop DC to back of work, sl last st. Turn.

Rep rows 41A–42B nine more times.

Row 61A: With LC, k1, *sl1yo, knit 1 st tog with the yo above it; rep from * to last 7 sts, (sl1yo, purl 1 st tog with the yo above it) 3 times, drop LC to front of work, sl last st. Do not turn work, slide sts to beg of row again.

Row 61B: With DC, sl 1 wyf, *purl 1 st tog with the yo above it, sl1yo; rep from * to last 5 sts, (knit 1 st tog with the yo above it, sl1yo) twice, k1. Turn.

Row 62A: With LC, sl 1 wyb, (knit 1 st tog with the yo above it, sl1yo) 3 times, *purl 1 st tog with the yo above it, sl1yo; rep from * to last st, p1. Do not turn work, slide sts to beg of row again.

Row 62B: With DC, p1, (sl1yo, purl 1 st tog with the yo above it) twice, *sl1yo, knit 1 st tog with the yo above it; rep from * to last st, drop DC to back of work, sl last st. Turn.

Rep rows 61A–62B nine more times.

Cont in this manner, syncopating 1 LC column and 1 DC column every 20 rows until all sts have been reversed. Work 20 more rows in the reversed patt. BO all sts.

finishing

Weave in ends.

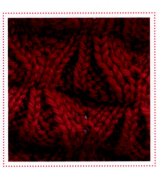

tiptoe through the tulips
LACE COWL

Dress up any outfit with this vibrant allover textured cowl. It's knit in the round in an intermediate lace pattern reminiscent of a field of flowers. If you'd like a longer cowl, simply add more repeats.

Designed by Angela Hahn

Finished Size

29½" (75 cm) circumference at base and 18½" (47 cm) circumference at top, slightly stretched; 6" (15 cm) wide.

Yarn

Worsted weight (#4 Medium).

Shown here: Cascade Yarns *Pacific* (40% superwash merino, 60% acrylic; 213 yd [195 m]/100 g): #53 beet, 1 skein.

Needles

Size U.S. 7 (4.5 mm): 16" or 24" (40 or 60 cm) circular (cir).

Adjust needle sizes if necessary to obtain the correct gauge.

Notions

Stitch marker; tapestry needle.

Gauge

About 26 sts and 29 rounds = 4" (10 cm) in lace chart, unblocked.

Note

This cowl was designed to be worn without blocking, to maintain the sculpted texture of the pattern stitch.

Cowl

CO 216 sts. Place marker (pm), and join for working in rnds, being careful not to twist sts.

Work rnds 1–42 of lace chart—120 sts rem after rnd 35. **Note:** Twenty-four stitches are decreased in each decrease round (2 stitches in each repeat) on rounds 2, 4, 6, and 34.

Rnd 43: BO all sts pwise.

Finishing

Weave in ends.

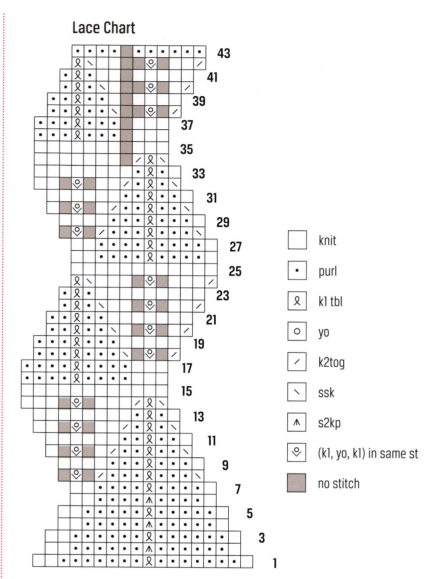

Lace Chart

☐	knit
•	purl
୧	k1 tbl
o	yo
/	k2tog
\	ssk
⋀	s2kp
⬙	(k1, yo, k1) in same st
▨	no stitch

NOTE: On rnds 17, 19, 21, 23, 37, 39, and 41, work in patt to last st, pm for beg of new rnd, not working last st (last st becomes first st of next rnd and is worked together with the next st). Remove the old beg-of-rnd marker before working the first k2tog of rnds 18, 20, 22, 24, 38, 40, and 42.

college prep
CABLED SHOULDER WARMER

Worked from the top down and knit in the round in stockinette stitch with a ribbed collar, this preppy shoulder warmer is a smart combination of short-row shaping and cables. The short-rows create a swooping asymmetrical curved edge while the cabling ensures a flattering fit across the shoulders and bust.

Designed by Robin Melanson

Finished Sizes

Neck circumference about 20½ (21½, 22¾, 23¾)" (52 [54.5, 58, 60.5] cm); circumference at lower edge about 52¾ (56¼, 62, 65½)" (134 [143, 157.5, 166.5] cm).

To fit approximate bust sizes 30–34 (36–40, 42–46, 48–52)" (76–86.5 [91.5–101.5, 106.5–117, 122–132] cm). Shown in size 30–34" (76–86.5 cm).

Yarn

Chunky weight (#5 Bulky).

Shown here: Cascade Yarns *Pacific Chunky* (40% superwash merino, 60% acrylic; 120 yd [110 m]/100 g): #71 little boy blue, 3 (3, 4, 4) skeins.

Needles

Size U.S. 10½ (6.5 mm): 16" and 32" (40 and 80 cm) long circular (cir).

Adjust needle size if necessary to obtain the correct gauge.

Notions

Cable needle (cn); stitch markers; tapestry needle.

Gauge

14 sts and 20 rows (or rnds) = 4" (10 cm) over St st.

Note

Stitch markers are used to indicate pattern placement; slip all markers as you come to them unless instructed otherwise.

Stitch Guide

3/3 LC (3 over 3 left cross): Slip next 3 sts onto cn and hold in front of work, k3, k3 from cn.

3/3 RC (3 over 3 right cross): Slip next 3 sts onto cn and hold in back of work, k3, k3 from cn.

4/4 LC (4 over 4 left cross): Slip next 4 sts onto cn and hold in front of work, k4, k4 from cn.

4/4 RC (4 over 4 right cross): Slip next 4 sts onto cn and hold in back of work, k4, k4 from cn.

K2, P2 RIB (MULTIPLE OF 4 STS)

Rnd 1: *K2, p2; rep from * to end.

Rep rnd 1 for patt.

Shoulder Warmer

With shorter cir needle, CO 80 (84, 88, 92) sts. Place marker (pm), join for working in rnds, being careful not to twist sts.

Work in k2, p2 rib until piece measures about 4" (10 cm) from beg.

Next rnd (setup): *K1, M1, [k2, M1] twice, k1, pm, p2, k10 (11, 12, 13), p2, pm; rep from * 3 more times, omitting final marker placement—92 (96, 100, 104) sts.

Inc rnd: *Work chart A over next 9 sts to m, p2, k1, LRI, knit to 3 sts before next m, LLI, k1, p2; rep from * 3 more times—8 sts inc'd.

Cont chart A between markers, and other sts as established, work new sts in St st. Rep inc rnd every other rnd 7 more times, ending with chart A rnd 7—156 (160, 164, 168) sts. **Note:** Change to longer cir needle when there are too many sts to work comfortably on shorter cir needle.

Next rnd (cable, inc): *K2, M1, [k3, M1] twice, k1, work to next m; rep from * 3 more times—168 (172, 176, 180) sts.

Beg chart B over sts between m and work 2 (2, 0, 0) rnds even.

Next rnd (inc): *Work chart B over next 12 sts to m, p2, k1, LRI, knit to 3 sts before next m, LLI, k1, p2; rep from * 3 more times—8 sts inc'd.

Rep inc rnd every 4 (4, 2, 2) rnds 3 (4, 2, 2) more times, then every 0 (0, 4, 4) rnds 0 (0, 4, 5) times—200 (212, 232, 244) sts.

Chart A

7
5
3
1

8-rnd rep

9-st rep

Chart B

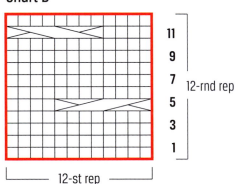

11
9
7
5
3
1

12-rnd rep

12-st rep

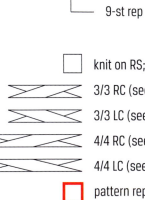

knit on RS; purl on WS

3/3 RC (see Stitch Guide)

3/3 LC (see Stitch Guide)

4/4 RC (see Stitch Guide)

4/4 LC (see Stitch Guide)

pattern rep

Work 2 rnds even. Piece measures about 6¾ (7½, 8, 8¾)" (17 [19, 20.5, 22] cm) from end of rib.

CURVED EDGE

Beg working back and forth using short-rows to shape lower edge (see Glossary).

Next row (RS): Work to last 3 sts, w&t.

Next row (WS): Work to 15 sts before beg of rnd marker, w&t.

Next row (RS): Work to 8 (9, 9, 10) sts before wrapped st on previous row, w&t.

Next row (WS): Work to 8 (9, 9, 10) sts before wrapped st on previous row, w&t.

Rep last 2 rows 9 more times—11 wrapped sts on each side.

With RS facing, work to end of rnd, then work next 100 (106, 116, 122) sts in established patt, working wraps tog with sts they wrap, ending at center of rnd. BO all sts pwise.

finishing

Weave in ends. Block to finished measurements.

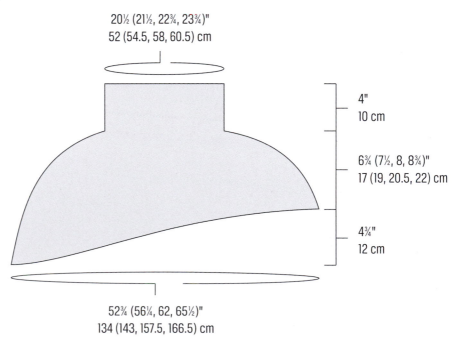

20½ (21½, 22¾, 23¾)"
52 (54.5, 58, 60.5) cm

4"
10 cm

6¾ (7½, 8, 8¾)"
17 (19, 20.5, 22) cm

4¾"
12 cm

52¾ (56¼, 62, 65½)"
134 (143, 157.5, 166.5) cm

twist & shout
CABLES AND GARTER-STITCH SCARF

This unisex scarf is a fantastic introduction to cabling. A quick four-stitch vertical cable pattern runs parallel to horizontal garter sections, creating a striking striped effect.

Designed by Tanis Gray

Finished Size

60½" (153.5 cm) long and 5½" (14 cm) wide.

Yarn

Chunky weight (#5 Bulky).

Shown here: Cascade Yarns *Pacific Chunky* (40% superwash merino, 60% acrylic; 120 yd [110 m]/100 g): #34 pewter, 2 skeins.

Needles

Size U.S. 10 (6 mm) needles.

Adjust needle size if necessary to obtain the correct gauge.

Notions

Cable needle (cn); tapestry needle.

Gauge

19 sts and 16 rows = 4" (10 cm) over cable chart.

Stitch Guide

2/2 LC (2 over 2 left cross): Sl next 2 sts onto cn and hold in front of work, k2, k2 from cn.

Scarf

CO 26 sts.

Knit 2 rows.

Work rows 1–8 of cable chart 30 times, or to desired length, leaving 2 yd (1.8 m) of yarn.

Knit 2 rows.

BO all sts kwise.

finishing

Weave in ends. Block to finished measurements.

Cable Chart

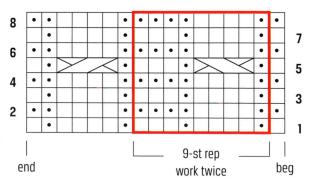

☐   knit on RS; purl on WS

•   purl on RS; knit on WS

✕   2/2 LC (see Stitch Guide)

▭   pattern rep

weekend away

LACE GAITER

This lace neckwarmer is a basic mix of increases, decreases, and stockinette stitch. It knits up swiftly in the round and takes only one skein of yarn, so bring this project on the plane or train with you to knit on your next weekend getaway.

Designed by Veronica Parsons

Finished Size

About 22½" (57 cm) circumference and 11½" (29 cm) wide.

Yarn

Worsted weight (#4 Medium).

Shown here: Cascade Yarns *Pacific* (40% superwash merino, 60% acrylic; 213 yd [195 m]/100 g): #16 spring green, 1 skein.

Needles

Size U.S. 8 (5 mm): 16" (40 cm) circular (cir).

Adjust needle size if necessary to obtain the correct gauge.

Notions

Stitch marker; tapestry needle.

Gauges

19 sts and 23½ rnds = 4" (10 cm) over chart B.

gaiter

CO 108 sts. Place marker (pm), and join to work in rnds, being careful not to twist sts.

Purl 1 rnd.

Knit 1 rnd.

Work rnds 1–11 of chart A.

Work rnds 1–8 of chart B 6 times.

Work rnds 1–11 of chart A once more.

Knit 1 rnd.

Purl 1 rnd.

BO loosely.

finishing

Weave in ends. Block to finished measurements.

knit

· purl

o yo

\ ssk

/ k2tog

pattern rep

Chart A

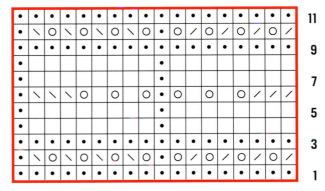

18-st rep

Chart B

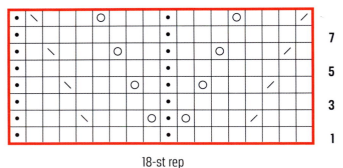

18-st rep

on the edge
TEXTURED CAPELET

This cabled, ribbed, and seed-stitch capelet combines a plethora of techniques for maximum texture. The asymmetrical bottom edge in a contrasting color is an unexpected touch.

Designed by Faina Goberstein

Finished Size

58" (147.5 cm) length at bottom curve, 22¼" (56.5 cm) along neckline curve, 34" (86.5 cm) cowl circumference, 10½" (26.5 cm) long side length, and 7¼" (18.5 cm) short side length.

Yarn

Worsted weight (#4 Medium).

Shown here: Cascade Yarns *Pacific* (40% merino wool, 60% acrylic; 213 yd [195 m]/100 g): #21 aquamarine (MC), 3 skeins; #43 ruby (CC), 1 skein.

Needles

Size U.S. 5 (3.75 mm): 16" (40 cm) and 32" (80 cm) circular (cir) and 1 double-pointed (dpn).

Adjust needle size if necessary to obtain the correct gauge.

Notions

Markers (m); cable needle (cn); three ⅞" (22 mm) buttons; tapestry needle.

Gauges

25 sts and 28 rows = 4" (10 cm) over cable chart.

20 sts and 26 rows = 4" (10 cm) over k2, p1 rib.

19 sts and 32 rows = 4" (10 cm) over seed st and stockinette stripes.

Notes

The front seed stitch bands are worked at the same time as the body of the cowl using the intarsia method to change colors.

Use a separate ball of yarn for each color area. On every row at at each color change, twist yarns to avoid a hole by laying the strand just worked over the strand to be worked.

art deco
FAUX CABLES SCARF

This elegant scarf is an effortless mix of knits and purls. By binding off stitches in the middle of the row to make an open space, a lacy faux cable design is created. The completely reversible pattern looks much more complex than it actually is.

Designed by Angela Tong

Finished Size

58" (147.5 cm) long and 6" (15 cm) wide.

Yarn

Chunky weight (#5 Bulky).

Shown here: Cascade Yarns *Pacific Chunky* (40% superwash merino, 60% acrylic; 120 yd [110 m]/100 g): #15 taupe, 2 skeins.

Needles

Size U.S. 10.5 (6.5 mm) needles.

Adjust needle size if necessary to obtain the correct gauge.

Notions

Tapestry needle.

Gauge

16 sts and 16 rows = 4" (10 cm) in blocks patt.

Note

Use backward-loop cast-on (see Glossary) when casting on new stitches.

Stitch Guide

BLOCKS PATTERN

Rows 1 and 3: K6, [p6, k3] twice.

Rows 2 and 4: K9, p3, k6, p3, k3.

Row 5: K3, sl 1 kwise, k2, psso, CO 4 sts, BO 5 sts pwise (1 st on RH needle after BO gap), CO 2 sts, BO 2 sts kwise (1 st on RH needle after BO gap), CO 5 sts, BO 4 sts pwise (1 st on RH needle after BO gap), CO 1 st, p1, k3.

Rep rows 1–5 for patt.

Scarf

CO 24 sts. Knit 4 rows.

Work rows 1–5 of Blocks Pattern 44 times, then work rows 1–4 once more.

Knit 4 rows. BO all sts kwise.

finishing

Weave in ends. Block to finished measurements.

final frost
LACE CAPELET

This pretty combination of lace flowers checkerboarded with reverse stockinette stitch gives a hint of spring even in the middle of winter. It's constructed from the bottom up and knit in the round, with a ribbed neck for warmth while chilly temps linger. Wear it loosely around the neck or pulled down over your shoulders for two different looks.

Designed by Linda Medina

Finished Sizes

Finished bust measurements: 37¾ (41¼, 44½, 51½)" (96 [105, 113, 131] cm) Shown in size 37¾" (96 cm).

Length, from neck: 11½ (12¼, 12¾, 13¼)" (29 [31, 32.5, 33.5] cm).

Yarn

Chunky weight (#5 Bulky).

Shown here: Cascade Yarns *Pacific Chunky* (40% superwash merino, 60% acrylic; 120 yd [110 m]/100 g): #23 dusty turquoise, 3 (3, 4, 4) skeins.

Needles

Size U.S. 10 (6 mm): 24" and 29" (60 and 74 cm) circular (cir).

Size U.S. 11 (8 mm): 16" (40 cm) circular (cir).

Adjust needle sizes if necessary to obtain the correct gauge.

Notions

Stitch marker; tapestry needle.

Gauge

14 sts and 20 rnds = 4" (10 cm) over stitch pattern.

Notes

Begin working with the longer circular needle and change to the shorter circular needle when there are too few stitches to work comfortably on the longer needle.

A stitch marker is used to mark the beginning of the round; slip the marker every round as you come to it.

Capelet

LOWER BORDER

With longer size 10 (6 mm) cir needle, CO 132 (144, 156, 180) sts. Place marker (pm), join for working in rnds, taking care not to twist sts.

Rnd 1: Purl.

Rnd 2: Knit.

Rep rnds 1 and 2 two (two, three, four) more times.

SIZES 37¾ (41¼)" (96 [105] CM) ONLY

Rep rnd 1 once more.

BODY

Rnd 1: *P3, k3, yo, s2kp, yo, k3; rep from * around.

Rnd 2 and all other even rnds: Knit the knit sts and yos, purl the purl sts.

Rnd 3: *P3, k1, k2tog, yo, k3, yo, ssk, k1; rep from * around.

Rnd 5: Rep rnd 1.

Rnd 7: Knit.

Rnd 9: *Yo, s2kp, yo, k3, p3, k3; rep from * around.

Rnd 11: *K3, yo, ssk, k1, p3, k1, k2tog, yo; rep from * around.

Rnd 13: Rep rnd 9.

Rnd 15: Knit.

Rnds 17-20: Rep rnds 1-4.

Rnd 21 (dec): *P3, ssk, k1, yo, s2kp, yo, k1, k2tog; rep from * around—110 (120, 130, 150) sts rem.

Rnd 23: Knit.

Rnd 25: *Yo, s2kp, yo, k2, p3, k2; rep from * around.

Rnd 27: *K3, yo, ssk, p3, k2tog, yo; rep from * around.

Rnd 29: Rep rnd 25.

Rnd 31: Knit.

Rnd 33: *P3, k2, yo, s2kp, yo, k2; rep from * around.

Rnd 35: *P3, k2tog, yo, k3, yo, ssk; rep from * around.

Rnd 37: Rep rnd 33.

Rnd 39: Knit.

Rnds 41-48: Rep rnds 25-32.

Rnd 49 (dec): *P2tog, p1, k2, yo, s2kp, yo, k2; rep from * around— 99 (108, 117, 135) sts rem.

Rnd 51: *P2, k2tog, yo, k3, yo, ssk; rep from * around.

Rnd 53 (dec): *P2tog, k2, yo, s2kp, yo, k2; rep from * around— 88 (96, 104, 120) sts rem.

Rnd 54: Rep rnd 2. End size 37¾" (96 cm) here.

SIZES 41¼ (44½, 51½)" (105 [113, 131] CM) ONLY

Rnd 55: Knit.

Rnd 57: *S2kp, yo, k2, p1, k2, yo; rep from * around.

Rnd 58: Rep rnd 2. End size 41¼" (105 cm) here.

SIZES 44½ (51½)" (113 [131] CM) ONLY

Rnd 59: *K2, yo, ssk, p1, k2tog, yo, k1; rep from * around. End size 44½" (113 cm) here.

SIZE 51½" (131 CM) ONLY

Rnd 60 (dec): *K2tog, k2, p1, k3; rep from * to last 8 sts, k2tog, k2, p1, k1, k2tog—104 sts rem.

NECKBAND

Rnd 1: *K2, p2; rep from * around.

Rep last rnd 8 (8, 10, 12) more times.

Change to larger cir needle. Work 9 (9, 11, 13) more rnds.

BO all sts in patt.

finishing

Weave in ends. Block to finished measurements.

mondrian
INTARSIA SCARF

This artful color block and garter-stitch design will bump you from an intarsia novice to an expert. Add some fringe to make it picture perfect!

Designed by Galina Carroll

Finished Size

6¼" (16 cm) wide and 46" (117 cm) long, without fringe. Fringe is 5" (12.5 cm) long.

Yarn

Worsted weight (#4 Medium).

Shown here: Cascade Yarns *Pacific* (40% superwash merino, 60% acrylic; 213 yd [195 m]/100 g): #21 aquamarine (MC), 1 skein; #36 Christmas red (A), 1 skein; #40 peacock (B), 1 skein; #51 honeysuckle pink (C), 1 skein; #25 burnt orange (D), 1 skein; #33 cactus (E), 1 skein; #12 yellow (F), 1 skein.

Needles

Size U.S. 7 (4.5 mm) needles.

Adjust needle size if necessary to obtain the correct gauge.

Notions

Tapestry needle.

Gauge

18½ sts and 25 rows = 4" (10 cm) over garter stitch.

Notes

This scarf is worked using the intarsia method to change colors. Use a separate ball of yarn for each color area. On every row at at each color change, twist yarns to avoid a hole by laying the strand just worked over the strand to be worked.

Slip the first stitch of every row with the yarn in front and knit the last stitch of every row. However, when changing colors at the beginning of a row, knit the first stitch of the first row with the new color.

Scarf

With MC, CO 30 sts.

Rows 1-5: Knit.

Row 6: With C k17, with MC k13.

Row 7: With MC k13, with C k17.

Rows 8-10: Rep rows 6 and 7 once, then rep row 6 once more.

Row 11: With MC k23, with F k7.

Row 12: With F k7, with MC k23.

Rows 13-16: Rep rows 11 and 12 twice more.

Row 17: With MC k10, with D k20.

Row 18: With D k20, with MC k10.

Rows 19-21: Rep rows 17 and 18 once, then rep row 17 once more.

Row 22: With B k13, with MC k17.

Row 23: With MC k17, with B k13.

Rows 24-29: Rep rows 22 and 23 three more times.

Rows 30 and 32: With A k19, with MC k11.

Row 31: With MC k11, with A k19.

Row 33: With MC k6, with C k24.

Row 34: With C k24, with MC k6.

Rows 35-37: Rep rows 33 and 34 once, then rep row 33 once more.

Rows 38 and 40: With A k24, with MC k6.

Row 39: With MC k6, with A k24.

Rows 41-55: With MC knit.

Row 56: With MC k23, with F k7.

Row 57: With F k7, with MC k23.

Rows 58-76: Rep rows 56 and 57 nine more times, then rep row 56 once more.

Row 77: With MC k19, with E k11.

Row 78: With E k11, with MC k19.

Rows 79 and 80: Rep rows 77 and 78.

Row 81: With B k16, with MC k14.

Row 82: With MC k14, with B k16.

Rows 83 and 84: Rep rows 81 and 82.

Row 85: With C k14, with MC k16.

Row 86: With MC k15, with C k14.

Rows 87-89: Rep rows 85 and 86 once, then rep row 85 once more.

Row 90: With MC k11, with A k19.

Row 91: With A k19, with MC k11.

Rows 92 and 93: Rep rows 90 and 91.

Rows 94 and 95: With MC knit.

Row 96: With MC k21, with D k9.

Row 97: With D k9, with MC k21.

Rows 98-113: Rep rows 96 and 97 eight more times.

Row 114: With A k15, with MC k15.

Row 115: With MC k15, with A k15.

Row 116: With MC k21, with E k9.

Row 117: With E k9, with MC k21.

Rows 118 and 119: Rep rows 116 and 117.

Row 120: With B k12, with MC k18.

Row 121: With MC k18, with B k12.

Rows 122-124: Rep rows 120 and 121, then rep row 120 once more.

Row 125: With MC k25, with C k5.

Row 126: With C k5, with MC k25.

Rows 127-153: Rep rows 125 and 126 thirteen times, then rep row 125 once more.

Rows 154 and 156: With MC k20, with F k10.

Row 155: With F k10, with MC k20.

Row 157: With MC k15, with D k15.

Row 158: With D k15, with MC k15.

Rows 159-166: Rep rows 157 and 158 four more times.

Row 167: With C k5, with MC k25.

Row 168: With MC k25, with C k5.

Rows 169-177: Rep rows 167 and 168 four more times, then rep row 167 once more.

Row 178: With A k5, with MC k25.

Row 179: With MC k25, with A k5.

Rows 180-195: Rep rows 178 and 179 eight more times.

Row 196: With MC k25, with C k5.

Row 197: With C k5, with MC k25.

Rows 198-208: Rep rows 196 and 197 five more times, then rep row 196 once more.

Row 209: With E k11, with MC k19.

Row 210: With MC k19, with E k11.

Rows 211-213: Rep rows 209 and 210 once, then rep row 209 once more.

Row 214: With MC k14, with A k16.

Row 215: With A k16, with MC k14.

Row 216: With D k22, with MC k8.

Row 217: With MC k8, with D k22.

Rows 218 and 219: Rep rows 216 and 217.

Row 220: With MC k18, with B k12.

Row 221: With B k12, with MC k18.

Rows 222–225: Rep rows 220 and 221 twice.

Row 226: With C k7, with MC k23.

Row 227: With MC k23, with C k7.

Rows 228–234: Rep rows 226 and 227 three times, then rep row 226 once more.

Rows 235–254: With MC knit.

Row 255: With F k14, with MC k16.

Row 256: With MC k16, with F k14.

Rows 257–260: Rep rows 255 and 256 twice.

Rows 261 and 263: With MC k12, with A k18.

Row 262: With A k18, with MC k12.

Row 264: With MC k22, with D k8.

Row 265: With D k8, with MC k22.

Rows 266–270: Rep rows 264 and 265 twice, then rep row 264 once more.

Row 271: With E k13, with MC k17.

Row 272: With MC k17, with E k13.

Rows 273 and 274: Rep rows 271 and 272.

Row 275: With MC k14, with B k16.

Row 276: With B k16, with MC k14.

Rows 277 and 278: Rep rows 275 and 276.

Row 279: With MC k5 sts, with C k25.

Row 280: With C k25, with MC k5.

Rows 281 and 282: Rep rows 279 and 280.

Rows 283–286: With MC knit.

BO all sts kwise.

finishing

Weave in ends. Block to finished measurements.

Cut 60 strands of yarn, each about 10" (25.5 cm) long as foll: 43 in MC, 2 in A, 8 in B, 4 in C, and 3 in E.

Using 1 strand of yarn for each fringe, attach fringe to each short end of scarf as foll: on one end, 2 MC, 4 B, 3 E, 4 B, 17 MC; on second end, 20 MC, 2 C, 2 A, 2 C, 4 MC. Trim fringe to even length.

slip-switch
TWO-COLOR NECK GAITER

This cozy gaiter will keep your neck toasty and can be tucked under a coat collar to keep drafts at bay. It's a simple knit that looks more complex because the position of the two colors is reversed. In the top half of the cowl, the light color dominates; in the lower half, the darker shade steps forward.

Designed by Lynn Wilson

Finished Size

29" (73.5 cm) circumference at lower edge and 24" (61 cm) circumference at upper edge, 10½" (26.5 cm) long.

Yarn

Chunky weight (#5 Bulky).

Shown here: Cascade Yarns *Pacific Chunky* (40% superwash merino, 60% acrylic; 120 yd [110 m]/100 g): #42 espresso (A), 2 skeins; #1 cream (B), 2 skeins.

Needles

Size U.S. 10½ (6.5 mm): 24" (60 cm) circular (cir).

Adjust needle size if necessary to obtain the correct gauge.

Notions

Stitch marker; tapestry needle.

Gauge

13½ sts and 26 rnds = 4" (10 cm) over slip-stitch patt 1 or 2.

Note

When slipping stitches, be careful not to pull yarn too tightly across slipped stitches.

Stitch Guide

SLIP-STITCH PATTERN 1

Rnd 1: With B, *p1, sl 1 wyf; rep from * to end.

Rnd 2: With B, *k1, p1; rep from * to end.

Rnds 3 and 4: With A, knit.

Rep rnds 1–4 for patt.

SLIP-STITCH PATTERN 2

Rnd 1: With A, *p1, sl 1 wyf; rep from * to end.

Rnd 2: With A, *k1, p1; rep from * to end.

Rnds 3 and 4: With B, knit.

Rep rnds 1–4 for patt.

Neck Gaiter

With A, CO 98 sts. Place marker (pm), and join for working in rnds, taking care not to twist sts.

Rnds 1 and 2: With A, purl.

Rnd 3: With B, knit.

*Work rnds 1–4 of slip-stitch patt 1, then work rnds 1–3 once more.

Next rnd (dec): Work rnd 4 and k2tog twice at beg of rnd—2 sts dec'd.

Rep from * twice more—92 sts rem.

Work 7 rnds even.

Next rnd (dec): With A, p2tog twice, purl to end—90 sts.

With B, knit 2 rnds even.

*Work rnds 1–4 of slip-stitch patt 2, then work rnds 1–3 once more.

Next rnd (dec): Work rnd 4 and k2tog twice at beg of rnd—2 sts dec'd.

Rep from * twice more—84 sts rem.

Work 3 rnds even.

Next rnd (dec): With B, p2tog twice, purl to end—82 sts.

Purl 2 rnds even.

With B, BO all sts kwise.

finishing

Weave in ends. Block to finished measurements if desired.

basket case
WOVEN-STITCH SCARF

Beginning knitters will go crazy for this simple basketweave scarf. An easy mix of knit and purl stitches, the allover texture is a nice showcase for the variegated yarn.

Designed by Janis Gray

Finished Size

55" (139.5 cm) long and 6¾" (17 cm) wide.

Yarn

Chunky weight (#5 Bulky).

Shown here: Cascade Yarns *Pacific Multi Chunky* (40% superwash merino, 60% acrylic; 120 yd [110 m]/100 g): #610 bluebird, 2 skeins.

Needles

Size U.S. 10 (6 mm) needles.

Adjust needle size if necessary to obtain the correct gauge.

Notions

Tapestry needle.

Gauge

15½ sts and 17½ rows = 4" (10 cm) over texture pattern.

Stitch Guide

TEXTURE PATTERN

Rows 1 and 5 (RS): Knit.

Rows 2 and 6 (WS): K1, p24, k1.

Row 3: (K2, p6) 3 times, k2.

Row 4: K1, (p1, k6, p1) 3 times, k1.

Row 7: K1, (p3, k2, p3) 3 times, k1.

Row 8: K4, (p2, k6) twice, p2, k4.

Rep rows 1–8 for patt.

Scarf

CO 26 sts.

Knit 2 rows.

Work rows 1–8 of texture pattern 30 times, or to desired length.

Knit 2 rows.

BO all sts kwise.

finishing

Weave in ends. Block to finished measurements.

Snuggly Sweaters, Shawls & Shrugs

Cold weather got you down? Cozy up with your needles and yarn and knit yourself a super-soft cover-up. From elegant designs in traditional styles to modern silhouettes that look marvelous on all shapes and sizes, you'll be ready for any season.

lovely in lilac
RIBBED SHRUG

Step into spring in this sweet shrug. Knit in one piece with no seaming, this top-down cover-up is worked in an allover 1x1 rib to the bottom. An eyelet row then leads into a ruffled rib pattern that provides a flared edge, and the cap sleeves are picked up and knit but not joined for added charm.

Designed by Elspeth Kursh

Finished Sizes

25 (27¾, 30½, 33, 35¾)" (63.5 [70.5, 77.5, 84, 91] cm) wide. Shown in size 25" (63.5 cm).

Yarn

Chunky weight (#5 Bulky).

Shown here: Cascade Yarns *Pacific Chunky* (40% superwash merino, 60% acrylic; 120 yd [110 m]/100 g): #26 lavender, 4 (5, 5, 6, 6) skeins.

Needles

Size U.S. 10½ (6.5 mm): straight or 32" (80 cm) circular (cir).

Adjust needle size if necessary to obtain the correct gauge.

Notions

6 removable or locking stitch markers; tapestry needle.

Gauge

18 sts and 17½ rows = 4" (10 cm) over k1, p1 rib patt.

Stitch Guide

K1, P1 RIB (MULTIPLE OF 2 STS + 1)

Row 1 (RS): K1, *p1, k1; rep from * to end.

Row 2 (WS): P1, *k1, p1; rep from * to end.

Rep rows 1 and 2 for patt.

RUFFLE RIB (MULTIPLE OF 3 STS + 1)

Row 1 (RS): K1, *p2, k1; rep from * to end.

Row 2 (WS): P1, *p1, k2; rep from * to end.

Rep rows 1 and 2 for patt.

Shrug

CO 113 (125, 137, 149, 161) sts. Do not join.

Work in k1, p1 rib until piece measures 6¾ (7, 7¾, 8½, 9¼)" (17 [18, 19.5, 21.5, 23.5] cm) from beg. Place marker (pm) at each end of last row.

Work as established until piece measures 15¼ (16, 17¼, 18½, 19¾)" (38.5 [40.5, 44, 47, 50] cm) from beg. Pm at each end of last row.

Work as established until piece measures 18 (19, 21, 23, 25)" (45.5 [48.5, 53.5, 58.5, 63.5] cm), ending with a WS row.

Next row (inc, RS): K1, *yo, p1, k1; rep from * to end—169 (187, 205, 223, 241) sts.

Work in ruffle rib for 4" (10 cm); piece should measure about 22 (23, 25, 27, 29)" (56 [58.5, 63.5, 68.5, 73.5] cm) from beg. BO all sts in patt.

SLEEVES

With RS facing, using markers as guides, pick up and knit 31 (33, 37, 39, 43) sts along side edge. Do not join

Work in k1, p1 rib until sleeve measures 4 (5, 6, 6½, 7)" (10 [12.5, 15, 16.5, 18] cm). BO all sts in patt.

Finishing

Weave in ends. Block gently to measurements. Sew side seams. Do not sew sleeves together.

checkmate
SLIP-STITCH SHAWL

This basic shawl features a bit of intrigue with slip-stitch purl colorwork running between sections of stockinette stitch. Worked from the center top out, it's finished off with an attached I-cord border running around the edge. This clever shawl will keep you wrapped in warmth all winter long.

Designed by Mary Beth Temple

Finished Size

30" (76 cm) long along center by 59" (150 cm) wide across top, including trim.

Yarn

Chunky weight (#5 Bulky).

Shown here: Cascade Yarns *Pacific Chunky* (40% superwash merino, 60% acrylic; 120 yd [110 m]/100 g): #30 latte (MC), 4 skeins; #44 Italian plum (CC), 2 skeins.

Needles

Size U.S. 11 (8 mm): 36" (91) or longer circular (cir) and set of 2 double-pointed (dpn).

Adjust needle size if necessary to obtain the correct gauge.

Notions

Removable stitch marker; tapestry needle.

Gauge

13½ sts and 19 rows = 4" (10 cm) in patt stitch.

Notes

Slip all stitches purlwise.

A removable marker is used to mark the center stitch; move the marker up as work progresses. Once the pattern is well established, the marker may be removed if desired.

Shawl

With cir needle and MC, CO 3 sts.

Row 1 (WS): Yo, purl to end—4 sts.

Row 2 (RS): Yo, k1, yo, k1, yo, k2—7 sts.

Row 3: Rep row 1—8 sts.

Row 4: Yo, k3, yo, k1, yo, k4—11 sts. Place marker (pm) on center st.

Row 5: Rep row 1—12 sts.

Row 6: Yo, knit to center st, yo, k1, yo, knit to end—15 sts.

Rows 7-9: Rep rows 5 and 6, then rep row 5 once more—20 sts.

Row 10: With CC, yo, k1, (sl 1 wyb, k1) to center st, yo, k1, yo, (k1, sl 1 wyb) to end—23 sts.

Row 11: Yo, knit the knit sts and slip the sl sts wyf—24 sts.

Row 12: With MC, rep row 6—27 sts.

Row 13: Rep row 1—28 sts.

Rows 14 and 15: Rep rows 12 and 13—32 sts.

Row 16: With CC, yo, sl 1 wyb, (k1, sl 1 wyb) to center st, yo, k1, yo, (sl 1 wyb, k1) to end—35 sts.

Row 17: Rep row 11—36 sts.

Change to MC, rep rows 6-17 until work measures 29" (73.5 cm) from beg along center, ending with a row 9 or 15 of patt; st count increases 3 sts every RS row, and 1 st every WS row. Place sts on waste yarn.

EDGING

With cir needle and MC, and with RS facing, pick up and knit 121 sts across top edge.

With dpn and CC, CO 3 sts.

Row 1: K3, sl 1 MC st from cir needle to left end of dpn, slide sts to right end of dpn.

Rows 2-4: K2, k2tog, sl 1 MC st from cir needle to left end of dpn, slide sts to right end of dpn.

Row 5: K2, k2tog, slide sts to right side of dpn.

Rep rows 1-5 for patt across upper edge until 1 MC st rem on cir needle; do not slip this st to dpn. Slide sts to right end of dpn.

POINT

Row 1: K3, slide sts to right end of dpn.

Row 2: K3, sl MC st from cir needle to left end of dpn, slide sts to right end of dpn.

Row 3: K2, k2tog, slide sts to right end of dpn.

Row 4: K3, slide sts to right end of dpn.

Return held sts to cir needle.

Row 5: K3, sl 1 MC st from cir needle to left end of dpn, slide sts to right end of dpn.

Row 6: K2, k2tog, sl 1 MC st from cir needle to left end of dpn, slide sts to right end of dpn.

Rep row 6 across side of shawl until center st at bottom point is next st on cir needle.

Rep rows 1-6, then rep row 6 across rem side of shawl until 1 MC st rem on cir needle; do not sl this st to dpn.

Rep rows 1-4. Cut yarn, leaving a 12" (30.5 cm) tail.

Finishing

Graft rem 3 sts to CO sts at beg of I-cord BO.

Weave in ends. Block to finished measurements.

back to basics
STOCKINETTE VEST

This classic stockinette-stitch vest will be your go-to piece for autumn. Worked from the bottom up and tipped with ribbing on the edges, it features generous armholes for movement and layering. Worn open or buttoned up, this vest looks smart on all shapes and sizes.

Designed by Loren Cherensky

Finished Sizes

32 (36, 40, 44)" (81.5 [91.5, 101.5, 112] cm) bust circumference. Shown in size 32" (81.5 cm).

Yarn

Chunky weight (#5 Bulky).

Shown here: Cascade Yarns *Pacific Chunky* (40% superwash merino, 60% acrylic; 120 yd [110 m]/100 g): #69 navy, 3 (3, 4, 4) skeins.

Needles

Size U.S. 11 (8 mm) needles.

Adjust needle size if necessary to obtain the correct gauge.

Notions

Tapestry needle; four ¾" (19 mm) buttons.

Gauge

12 sts and 17 rows = 4" (10 cm) over St st.

Right front

CO 17 (20, 23, 26) sts.

Row 1 (WS): *K2, p2; rep from * to last 1 (0, 3, 2) st(s), p1 (0, 2, 2), k0 (0, 1, 0).

Row 2 (inc): P1f&b 1 (0, 0, 1) time, p0 (0, 0, 1), k1f&b 0 (1, 1, 0) time, k0 (1, 0, 0), p0 (2, 2, 0), *k2, p2; rep from * to end—1 st inc'd.

Rep last 2 rows 6 more times, working inc sts into rib patt—24 (27, 30, 33) sts. Piece should measure about 3¼" (8.5 cm).

Next row (WS): Purl.

Next row: Knit.

Cont in St st until piece measures 9½" (24 cm) from beg, ending with a RS row.

SHAPE ARMHOLE

BO at beg of WS rows 4 sts once, 3 sts once, then 1 st 2 (3, 4, 5) times. At the same time, when piece measures 9¾ (10, 10¼, 10½)" (25 [25.5, 26, 26.5] cm) from beg, end with a WS row.

SHAPE NECK

Next row (RS): Ssk, knit to end—1 st dec'd at neck edge.

Cont armhole shaping and rep dec at neck edge every 2 rows 0 (1, 2, 3) time(s), then every 4 rows 8 times—6 (7, 8, 9) sts rem when all shaping is complete.

Work even until piece measures 18¼ (19, 19¾, 20½)" (46.5 [48.5, 50, 52] cm) from beg. BO rem sts.

Left front

CO 17 (20, 23, 26) sts.

Row 1 (WS): K1 (0, 0, 2), p2 (2, 1, 2), *k2, p2; rep from * to last 2 sts, k2.

Row 2 (inc): *P2, k2; rep from * to last 1 (4, 3, 2) st(s), p0 (2, 2, 1), p1f&b 1 (0, 0, 1) time, k0 (1, 0, 0), k1f&b 0 (1, 1, 0) time—1 st inc'd.

Rep last 2 rows 6 more times, working inc sts into rib patt—24 (27, 30, 33) sts. Piece should measure about 3¼" (8.5 cm).

Next row (WS): Purl.

Next row: Knit.

Cont in St st until piece measures 9½" (24 cm) from beg, ending with a WS row.

SHAPE ARMHOLE

BO at beg of RS rows 4 sts once, 3 sts once, then 1 st 2 (3, 4, 5) times. At the same time, when piece measures 9¾ (10, 10¼, 10½)" (25 [25.5, 26, 26.5] cm) from beg, end with a WS row.

SHAPE NECK

Next row (RS): Work to last 2 sts, k2tog—1 st dec'd at neck edge.

Cont armhole shaping and rep dec at neck edge every 2 rows 0 (1, 2, 3) time(s), then every 4 rows 8 times—6 (7, 8, 9) sts rem when all shaping is complete.

Work even until piece measures 18¼ (19, 19¾, 20½)" (46.5 [48.5, 50, 52] cm) from beg. BO rem sts.

Back

CO 48 (54, 60, 66) sts.

Row 1 (WS): *K2, p2; rep from * to last 0 (2, 0, 2) sts, k0 (2, 0, 2).

Row 2: P0 (2, 0, 2), *k2, p2; rep from * to end.

Rep rows 1 and 2 six more times; rib should measure about 3¼" (8.5 cm).

Next row (WS): Purl.

Next row: Knit.

Cont in St st until piece measures 9½" (24 cm) from beg, ending with a WS row.

SHAPE ARMHOLES

BO 4 sts at beg of next 2 rows, then 3 sts at beg of next 2 rows. Dec 1 st each end every RS row 2 (3, 4, 5) times—30 (34, 38, 42) sts.

Work even until armhole measures 7 (7¾, 8½, 9¼)" (18 [19.5, 21.5, 23.5] cm), ending with a WS row.

SHAPE NECK

Next row (RS): K10 (11, 12, 13), join a second skein of yarn and BO 10 (12, 14, 16) sts for neck, work to end—10 (11, 12, 13) sts rem for each shoulder. Work both sides at same time with separate skeins of yarn. BO at each neck edge every other row 2 sts twice—6 (7, 8, 9) sts rem each shoulder. Work even until piece measures 18¼ (19, 19¾, 20½)" (46.5 [48.5, 50, 52] cm) from beg. BO rem sts.

finishing

Weave in ends. Block to finished measurements. Sew shoulder seams.

ARMHOLE RIBBING

With RS facing, pick up and knit 76 (80, 84, 88) sts along armhole.

Row 1 (WS): K1, *p2, k2; rep from * to last 3 sts, p2, k1.

Row 2: P1, *k2, p2; rep from * to last 3 sts, k2, p1.

Rep rows 1 and 2 until rib measures 1¼" (3.2 cm). BO all sts in rib patt. Rep on other armhole. Sew side seams.

FRONT AND NECK RIBBING

With RS facing, pick up and knit 73 (76, 79, 82) sts evenly along right front edge, 28 (30, 32, 34) sts along back neck edge, then 73 (76, 79, 82) sts along left front edge—174 (182, 190, 198) sts.

Row 1 (WS): P2, *k2, p2; rep from * to end.

Row 2: *K2, p2; rep from * to last 2 sts, k2.

Row 3: Rep row 1.

Row 4 (buttonhole): Work 12 sts in rib patt, (BO 1 st for buttonhole, work 8 [9, 10, 11] sts in rib patt) twice, BO 1 st, work in rib to end.

Row 5: CO 1 st over each BO st.

BO all sts.

Sew buttons to left front opposite buttonholes.

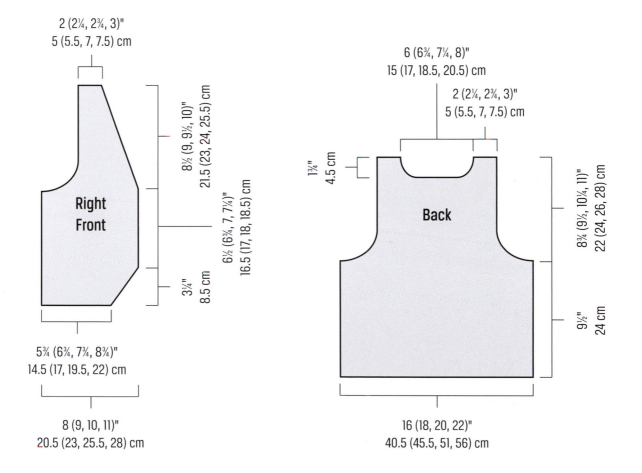

Right Front

2 (2¼, 2¾, 3)"
5 (5.5, 7, 7.5) cm

8½ (9, 9½, 10)"
21.5 (23, 24, 25.5) cm

6½ (6¾, 7, 7¼)"
16.5 (17, 18, 18.5) cm

3¼"
8.5 cm

5¾ (6¾, 7¾, 8¾)"
14.5 (17, 19.5, 22) cm

8 (9, 10, 11)"
20.5 (23, 25.5, 28) cm

Back

6 (6¾, 7¼, 8)"
15 (17, 18.5, 20.5) cm

2 (2¼, 2¾, 3)"
5 (5.5, 7, 7.5) cm

1¾"
4.5 cm

8¾ (9½, 10¼, 11)"
22 (24, 26, 28) cm

9½"
24 cm

16 (18, 20, 22)"
40.5 (45.5, 51, 56) cm

a good ribbing
BRIOCHE PULLOVER

This brioche-ribbed pullover is a sumptuous blend of texture and coziness. The sleeve cuffs are worked vertically, then rotated with stitches picked up to work the sleeves. The oversized turtleneck will keep your neck extra warm.

Designed by Debbie O'Neill

Finished Sizes

31½ (35, 38¾, 42½, 46¼, 49¾)" (80 [89, 98.5, 108, 117.5, 126.5] cm) bust circumference. Shown in size 31½" (80 cm).

Yarn

Chunky weight (#5 Bulky).

Shown here: Cascade Yarns *Pacific Chunky* (40% superwash merino, 60% acrylic; 120 yd [110 m]/100 g): #73 denim, 8 (9, 10, 11, 12, 13) skeins.

Needles

Size U.S. 9 (5.5 mm): straight and 16" (40 cm) circular (cir).

Adjust needle size if necessary to obtain the correct gauge.

Notions

Stitch holders; stitch marker; tapestry needle.

Gauge

13 sts and 20 rows = 4" (10 cm) over brioche rib stitch before blocking. Fabric will relax with blocking.

Note

This fabric is extremely elastic and can be stretched to a wide range of widths or lengths. When choosing which size to knit, err on the smaller side.

Back

With straight needles, CO 57 (63, 69, 75, 81, 87) sts. Work in brioche rib in rows for 5 (5, 6, 6, 7, 7)" (12.5 [12.5, 15, 15, 18, 18] cm), ending with a WS row.

SHAPE WAIST

Next row (RS): K2tog, work in established brioche rib patt to last 2 sts, k2tog—2 sts dec'd.

Work 3 rows even.

Rep rows 1–4 three more times—49 (55, 61, 67, 73, 79) sts rem.

Work 4 (4, 6, 6, 8, 8) rows even.

Next row (RS): K1, M1, work in established brioche rib patt to last st, M1, k1—2 sts inc'd.

Work 3 rows even.

Rep last 4 rows once more—53 (59, 65, 71, 77, 83) sts total.

Cont even until piece measures 15 (16, 17, 18, 19, 20)" (38 [40.5, 43, 45.5, 48.5, 51] cm) from beg, ending with a WS row.

SHAPE ARMHOLES

BO 4 sts at beg of next 2 rows. Dec 1 st each end of every RS row 4 (4, 4, 6, 6, 6) times—37 (43, 49, 51, 57, 63) sts rem. Cont even until armhole measures 6 (6½, 7, 7½, 8, 8½)" (15 [16.5, 18, 19, 20.5, 21.5] cm), ending with a WS row.

SHAPE NECK AND SHOULDERS

Next row (RS): Work 10 (12, 14, 14, 16, 18) sts, BO center 17 (19, 21, 23, 25, 27) sts in patt, work to end—10 (12, 14, 14, 16, 18) sts rem for each shoulder. Place rem sts on holders.

Front

Work as for back until armhole measures 2" (5 cm), ending with a WS row. Mark center 11 (13, 15, 17, 19, 21) sts for neck.

SHAPE NECK

Next row (RS): Cont rem armhole dec and work to marker, join a second skein of yarn and BO marked sts in patt, work to end of row. Cont each side separately.

BO every other row at each neck edge 2 sts once, then 1 st once—10 (12, 14, 14, 16, 18) sts rem each side. Work even until front measures same length as back. Place rem sts on holders.

Sleeves (make 2)

With straight needles, CO 15 sts. Work in brioche rib in rows until piece measures 10 (11, 12, 13, 14, 15)" (25.5 [28, 30.5, 33, 35.5, 38] cm), ending with a WS row. BO all sts in patt, leaving last st on needle.

With RS facing, pick up and knit 32 (36, 40, 44, 48, 50) sts along long edge of piece—33 (37, 41, 45, 49, 53) sts total. Work 3 (3, 3, 5, 5, 5) rows in brioche rib.

Next row (inc, RS): K1, M1, work in patt to last st, M1, k1—2 sts inc'd.

Rep inc row every 4 (4, 6, 6, 6, 6) rows 5 more times—45 (49, 53, 57, 61, 65) sts. Work even until piece measures 12 (12, 12½, 12½, 13, 13)" (30.5 [30.5, 32, 32, 33, 33] cm) from bottom edge, ending with a WS row.

SHAPE CAP

Dec 1 st each end of every 4 rows 4 (4, 4, 6, 6, 6) times—37 (41, 45, 45, 49, 53) sts rem. BO all sts in patt.

Finishing

Join shoulders using three-needle bind-off (see Glossary). Sew sleeves into armholes, working from shoulder seam to underarm. Sew side seams, working from hem to underarm. Sew sleeve seams, working from cuff to underarm.

COLLAR

With cir needle and RS facing, beg at shoulder seam, pick up and knit 66 (76, 86, 96, 106, 116) sts along neck edge. Place marker (pm) for beg of rnd and join for knitting in rnd. Work brioche rib in rounds for 7 (7, 7, 8, 8, 8)" (18 [18, 18, 20.5, 20.5, 20.5] cm), or to desired length. BO all stitches in patt.

Weave in ends. Wash and block to finished measurements.

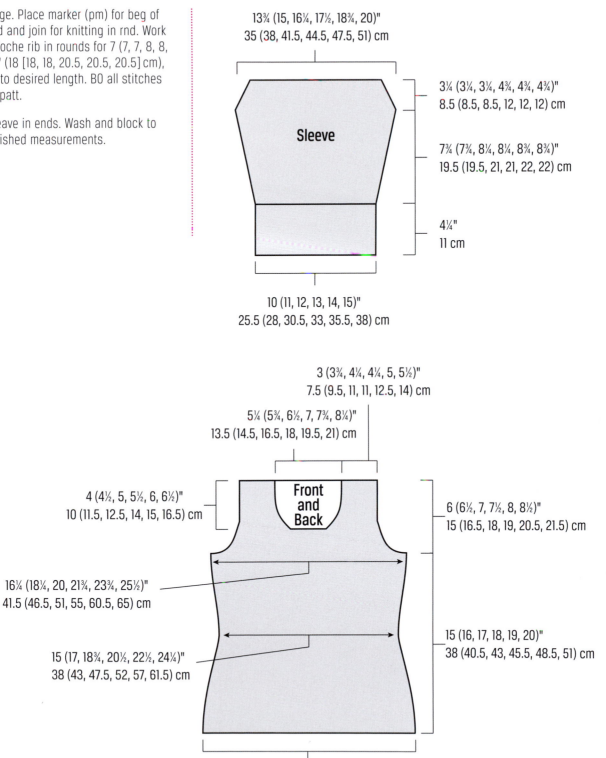

13¾ (15, 16¼, 17½, 18¾, 20)"
35 (38, 41.5, 44.5, 47.5, 51) cm

3¼ (3¼, 3¼, 4¾, 4¾, 4¾)"
8.5 (8.5, 8.5, 12, 12, 12) cm

Sleeve

7¾ (7¾, 8¼, 8¼, 8¾, 8¾)"
19.5 (19.5, 21, 21, 22, 22) cm

4¼"
11 cm

10 (11, 12, 13, 14, 15)"
25.5 (28, 30.5, 33, 35.5, 38) cm

3 (3¾, 4¼, 4¼, 5, 5½)"
7.5 (9.5, 11, 11, 12.5, 14) cm

5¼ (5¾, 6½, 7, 7¾, 8¼)"
13.5 (14.5, 16.5, 18, 19.5, 21) cm

4 (4½, 5, 5½, 6, 6½)"
10 (11.5, 12.5, 14, 15, 16.5) cm

Front and Back

6 (6½, 7, 7½, 8, 8½)"
15 (16.5, 18, 19, 20.5, 21.5) cm

16¼ (18¼, 20, 21¾, 23¾, 25½)"
41.5 (46.5, 51, 55, 60.5, 65) cm

15 (16, 17, 18, 19, 20)"
38 (40.5, 43, 45.5, 48.5, 51) cm

15 (17, 18¾, 20½, 22½, 24¼)"
38 (43, 47.5, 52, 57, 61.5) cm

17½ (19½, 21¼, 23, 25, 26¾)"
44.5 (49.5, 54, 58.5, 63.5, 68) cm

red hot
TEXTURED SHRUG

Worked flat in moss stitch framed by cables, this shrug is then folded and seamed to create sleeves. Ribbed cuffs and edging are added at the very end by picking up along the openings and knitting out. The ribbing provides an interesting contrast to the textured moss stitch and smooth cabling.

Designed by Robin Melanson

Finished Sizes

Piece measures about 20¾ (23½, 25¼, 28¾)" (52.5 [59.5, 64, 73] cm) wide by 45 (49, 53, 57)" (114.5 [124.5, 134.5, 145] cm) long, before folding.

To fit approximate bust sizes 30–34 (36–40, 42–46, 48–52)" (76–86.5 [91.5–101.5, 106.5–117, 122–132] cm). Shown in size 30–34" (76–86.5 cm).

Yarn

Chunky weight (#5 Bulky).

Shown here: Cascade Yarns *Pacific Chunky* (40% superwash merino, 60% acrylic; 120 yd [110 m]/100 g): #43 ruby, 6 (8, 9, 11) skeins.

Needles

Size U.S. 10½ (6.5 mm): 32" (80 cm) circular (cir) and set of 5 double-pointed (dpn).

Adjust needle size if necessary to obtain the correct gauge.

Notions

Cable needle (cn); stitch markers; tapestry needle.

Gauge

15 sts and 19 rows = 4" (10 cm) over moss stitch.

2/2 LC (2 over 2 left cross): Slip next 2 sts onto cn and hold in front of work, k2, k2 from cn.

2/2 RC (2 over 2 right cross): Slip next 2 sts onto cn and hold in back of work, k2, k2 from cn.

MOSS STITCH (ODD NUMBER OF STS)

Row 1 (RS): K1, *p1, k1; rep from * to end.

Rows 2 and 3: P1, *k1, p1; rep from * to end.

Row 4: K1, *p1, k1; rep from * to end.

Rep rows 1–4 for patt.

K2, P2 RIB (WORKED IN THE RND; MULTIPLE OF 4 STS)

Rnd 1: *K2, p2; rep from * to end.

Rep rnd 1 for patt.

Shrug

With cir needle, CO 81 (91, 101, 111) sts. Do not join; work back and forth in rows.

Row 1 (RS): K1, work row 1 of cable chart over next 8 sts, place marker (pm), work in moss st to last 9 sts, pm, work row 1 of cable chart over next 8 sts, k1.

Row 2 (WS): P1, work row 2 of cable chart over next 8 sts, sm, work in moss st to next m, sm, work row 2 of cable chart over next 8 sts, k1.

Cont in established patt until piece measures about 45 (49, 53, 57)" (114.5 [124.5, 134.5, 145] cm) long.

BO all sts in patt.

Finishing

Weave in ends. Block to finished measurements. Fold shrug as shown in diagram and sew together where indicated.

CUFFS

With dpns and RS facing, beg at seam of cuff opening, pick up and knit 28 (36, 40, 48) sts around cuff opening. Distribute sts evenly over 4 dpn. Pm for beg of rnd and join for working in rnds.

Work in k2, p2 rib until cuff measures about 4½" (11.5 cm) long. BO loosely in patt.

EDGING

With cir needle and RS facing, beg at right arm seam (longer edge will be at left side of work), pick up and knit 102 (110, 122, 126) sts evenly along upper front and neck edge to left arm seam, and 38 (42, 46, 50) sts evenly along lower back edge (about 1 stitch for every 2 rows along entire edge)—140 (152, 168, 176) sts. Pm for beg of rnd, and join for working in rnds.

Work in k2, p2 rib for about 2¼" (5.5 cm). BO loosely in patt.

Cable Chart

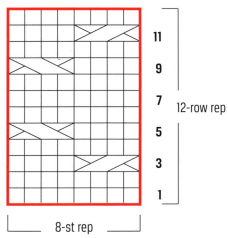

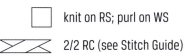

knit on RS; purl on WS

2/2 RC (see Stitch Guide)

2/2 LC (see Stitch Guide)

pattern rep

front and neck edge

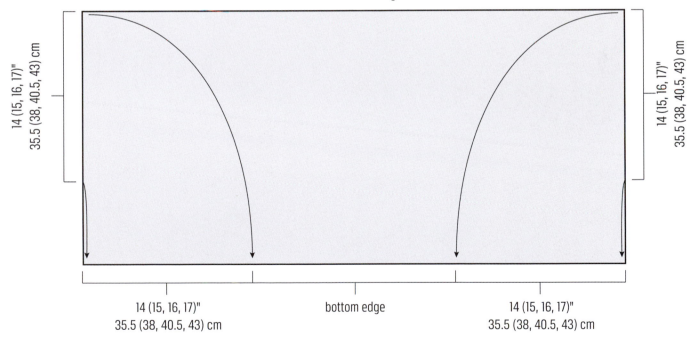

14 (15, 16, 17)"
35.5 (38, 40.5, 43) cm

14 (15, 16, 17)"
35.5 (38, 40.5, 43) cm

14 (15, 16, 17)"
35.5 (38, 40.5, 43) cm

bottom edge

14 (15, 16, 17)"
35.5 (38, 40.5, 43) cm

NOTE: Fold sides down to bottom edge in direction of arrows and sew together.

victorian lady
LACE-BORDER SHAWL

This elegant wrap is worked from the outside in, beginning with the lace border, and shaped with short-rows in stockinette stitch with decreases on either side. The chunky yarn knits up quickly, just in time for high tea!

Designed by Hilary Smith Callis

Finished Size

21" (53.5 cm) wide × 52" (132 cm) long.

Yarn

Chunky weight (#5 Bulky).

Shown here: Cascade Yarns *Pacific Chunky* (40% superwash merino, 60% acrylic; 120 yd [110 m]/100 g): #20 baby blue, 3 skeins.

Needles

Size U.S. 11 (8 mm): 40" to 60" (100 to 150 cm) circular (cir).

Adjust needle size if necessary to obtain the correct gauge.

Notions

Tapestry needle.

Gauge

11½ sts and 15½ rows = 4" (10 cm) over stockinette stitch.

12 sts and 15 rows = 4" (10 cm) over vine lace border patt.

Shawl

CO 193 sts. Do not join.

Knit 1 row.

BEGIN VINE LACE BORDER

Row 1 (RS): K3, *yo, k2, ssk, k2tog, k2, yo, k1; rep from * to last st, k1.

Rows 2 and 4 (WS): K1, purl to last st, k1.

Row 3: K2, *yo, k2, ssk, k2tog, k2, yo, k1; rep from * to last 2 sts, k2.

Rows 5–18: Rep rows 1–4 three more times, then rep rows 1 and 2 once more.

SHAPE SHAWL

Short-row 1 (RS): K99, k2tog, k2, turn—1 st dec'd.

Short-row 2 (WS): Sl 1, p7, ssp, p2, turn—1 st dec'd.

Short-row 3: Sl 1, knit to 1 st before turn on last row, k2tog, k2, turn—1 st dec'd.

Short-row 4: Sl 1, purl to 1 st before turn on last row, ssp, p2, turn work—1 st dec'd.

Rep last 2 short-rows 28 more times, then rep short-row 3 once more—132 sts. **Note:** The last row should take you to the end of the row on the RS.

Next row (WS): Knit to 1 st before turn on last row, ssk, k2—131 sts. All sts have been worked.

BO all sts kwise.

finishing

Weave in ends.

Wash shawl and block to finished measurements, being sure to stretch vine lace border a bit to open it up.

flower girl
LACE AND STOCKINETTE SHELL

A dainty lace flower pattern creates a pretty and feminine design. Knit entirely in one piece with garter-stitch edging and no seaming, this effortless shell works up so quickly, you'll want to make one in every color in the garden.

Designed by Mary Beth Temple

Finished Sizes

31½ (36¾, 42¼, 47½, 52¾)" (80 [93.5, 107.5, 120.5, 134] cm) bust circumference. Shown in size 31½" (80 cm).

Yarn

Chunky weight (#5 Bulky).

Shown here: Cascade Yarns *Pacific Chunky* (40% superwash merino, 60% acrylic; 120 yd [110 m]/100 g): #16 spring green, 4 (4, 5, 5, 6) skeins.

Needles

Size U.S. 11 (8 mm): 16" and 36" (40 and 91 cm) or longer circular (cir).

Adjust needle size if necessary to obtain the correct gauge.

Notions

7 stitch markers; 2 long stitch holders or waste yarn; tapestry needle.

Gauge

12 sts and 16 rows = 4" (10 cm) over lace chart.

jane austen
LACE PANEL SHRUG

This sweetly feminine shrug is surprisingly quick and easy to knit. It's worked flat in an allover lace pattern with garter-stitch edging. Crocheted loops are added after blocking, and ribbon is pulled through and tied to create arm openings—no seaming required.

Designed by Elena Malo

Finished Sizes

30½ (34, 37½)" (77.5 [86.5, 95.5] cm) wide × 18 (20, 22)" (45.5 [51, 56] cm) long.

Yarn

Worsted weight (#4 Medium).

Shown here: Cascade Yarns *Pacific* (40% superwash merino, 60% acrylic; 213 yd [195 m]/100 g): #49 dark teal, 3 skeins.

Needles

Size U.S. 8 (5 mm) needles.

Adjust needle size if necessary to obtain the correct gauge.

Notions

Size G/6 (4 mm) crochet hook; tapestry needle; Offray Lady Chiffon ribbon (offray.com): #343 tornado, 1 spool.

Gauge

18 sts and 26 rows = 4" (10 cm) over lace patt.

Shrug

CO 137 (153, 169) sts. Knit 3 rows, ending with a WS row.

Work 16 rows of lace chart until piece measures about 17½ (19½, 21½)" (44.5 [49.5, 54.5] cm), ending with row 8 or 16.

Knit 3 rows.

BO all sts kwise on WS.

Finishing

Weave in ends. Block very lightly to finished measurements.

LOOPS

Cut 4 pieces of yarn, each 31" (78.5 cm) long. With crochet hook and WS facing, count 28 (31, 34) sts along CO edge. Insert hook in next st, fold 1 length of cut yarn in half and pull up a loop, working with both strands together tightly, ch 5; remove hook from last loop, skip 2 sts along CO edge, insert hook in next knit st, pull both strands through, fasten off. Rep on other end, inserting hook 31 (34, 37) sts from edge.

Rep on BO edge, counting 18 (21, 24) sts from first end and 21 (24, 27) sts from other end. Cut 2 pieces of ribbon, each 35" (89 cm) long. Slip each piece of ribbon through a front and back loop and tie in a bow.

Lace Chart

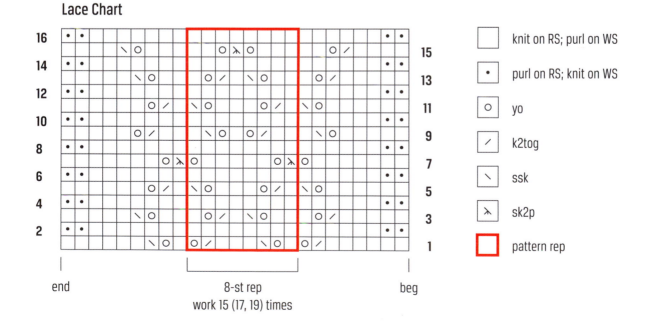

knit on RS; purl on WS

• purl on RS; knit on WS

○ yo

╱ k2tog

╲ ssk

⅄ sk2p

▢ pattern rep

end

8-st rep
work 15 (17, 19) times

beg

make mine mocha
STOCKINETTE PONCHO

Worked flat in one piece in stockinette stitch, this one-size-fits-all cover-up has swing and sass. Garter-stitch detailing around the borders and neck opening adds a touch of texture. Slip it on and head to your favorite café.

Designed by Loren Cherensky

Finished Size

41¼" (105 cm) wide and 27" (68.5 cm) long from shoulder.

Yarn

Chunky weight (#5 Bulky).

Shown here: Cascade Yarns *Pacific Chunky* (40% superwash merino, 60% acrylic; 120 yd [110 m]/100 g): #59 milk chocolate, 10 skeins.

Needles

Size U.S. 11 (8 mm) needles.

Adjust needle sizes if necessary to obtain the correct gauge.

Notions

Stitch holder; tapestry needle.

Gauge

12 sts and 16 rows = 4" (10 cm) over St st.

Poncho

FRONT

CO 124 sts. Work 3" (7.5 cm) in garter st (knit every row), ending with a RS row.

Next row (WS): K8, p108, k8.

Next row: Knit.

Rep last 2 rows until piece measures 22½" (57 cm) from beg, ending with a WS row.

SHAPE FRONT NECK BORDER
Row 1 (RS): Knit.

Row 2: K8, p30, k48, p30, k8.

Rep rows 1 and 2 rows until neck border measures 3" (7.5 cm), ending with a WS row.

SHAPE NECK
Next row (RS): K49, place sts on holder for right shoulder, BO center 26 sts, knit to end—49 sts rem for left shoulder.

Next row (WS): K8, p30, k11.

Next row: Knit.

Rep last 2 rows until shoulder measures 3" (7.5 cm), ending with a WS row. Place sts on holder. Return held 49 sts for right shoulder to needles.

Next row (WS): K11, p30, k8.

Next row: Knit.

Rep last 2 rows until shoulder measures 3" (7.5 cm), ending with a WS row.

SHAPE NECK BORDER
Next row (RS): K49, CO 26 sts, k49 sts from holder—124 sts.

Work in garter st until neck border measures 3" (7.5 cm), ending with a WS row.

BACK
Next row (RS): Knit.

Next row: K8, p108, k8.

Rep last 2 rows until piece measures 51" (129.5 cm) from beg, ending with a WS row.

Work 3" (7.5 cm) in garter st. BO all sts kwise.

Finishing

Weave in ends. Block to finished measurements.

braided beauty

BELTED VEST

Cable detailing runs up the front opening of this stockinette vest with a ribbed hem. The four-stitch cable is worked as you go and neatly conceals the neck shaping. The finishing touch is a thickly braided belt, which is easily adjusted to your desired length.

Designed by Elspeth Kursh

Finished Sizes

32 (34½, 35½, 37½, 40, 42½, 44½)" (81.5 [87.5, 90, 95.5, 101.5, 108, 113] cm) bust circumference. Shown in size 32" (81.5 cm).

Yarn

Chunky weight (#5 Bulky).

Shown here: Cascade Yarns *Pacific Chunky* (40% superwash merino, 60% acrylic; 120 yd [110 m]/100 g): #30 latte, 5 (5, 5, 5, 6, 6, 6) skeins.

Needles

Size U.S. 10½ (6.5 mm): straight or 24" (60 cm) circular (cir).

Adjust needle size if necessary to obtain the correct gauge.

Notions

Cable needle (cn); tapestry needle.

Gauge

14 sts and 17 rows = 4" (10 cm) over St st.

K2, P2 RIB (MULTIPLE OF 4 STS + 1)

Row 1 (RS): K1, *p2, k2, rep from * to end.

Row 2 (WS): *P2, k2 rep from * to last st, p1.

Rep rows 1 and 2 for patt.

CABLE PATTERN (MULTIPLE OF 4 STS)

Row 1 (RS): Sl next 2 sts onto cn and hold in front of work, k1, k2 from cn, k1.

Row 2 and all WS rows: P4.

Row 3: K1, sl next st onto cn and hold in back of work, k2, k1 from cn.

Rep rows 1–3 for patt.

Back

CO 58 (62, 64, 68, 72, 76, 80) sts.

Work in k2, p2 rib for 1" (2.5 cm), ending with a WS row.

Cont in St st until piece measures 13 (13, 14, 14, 15, 15, 16)" (33 [33, 35.5, 35.5, 38, 38, 40.5] cm) from beg, ending with a WS row.

SHAPE ARMHOLES

BO 7 (8, 8, 9, 11, 11, 13) sts at beg of next 2 rows—44 (46, 48, 50, 50, 54, 54) sts rem.

Work even until piece measures 21 (21, 23, 23, 25, 25, 27)" (53.5 [53.5, 58.5, 58.5, 63.5, 63.5, 68.5] cm) from beg, ending with a WS row.

BO all sts.

Right Front

CO 36 (38, 40, 42, 44, 46, 48) sts.

Row 1 (RS): K4 (6, 4, 6, 4, 6, 4), *p2, k2; rep from * to end of row.

Row 2 (WS): *P2, k2; rep from * to last 4 (6, 4, 6, 4, 6, 4) sts, purl to end of row.

Rep rows 1 and 2 until rib measures 1" (2.5 cm), ending with a WS row.

Next row (setup, RS): Work row 1 of cable patt over first 4 sts, knit to end of row.

Next row: Purl to last 4 sts, work row 2 of cable patt over last 4 sts.

Note: Read over next section carefully as armhole and front neck shaping are worked at the same time.

Cont as established until piece measures 8 (8, 9, 9, 10, 10, 11)" (20.5 [20.5, 23, 23, 25.5, 25.5, 28] cm) from beg, ending with a WS row.

SHAPE NECK

Next row (dec, RS): Work next row of cable patt over first 4 sts, ssk, knit to end—1 st dec'd.

Next row: Purl.

Rep last 2 rows 9 (9, 10, 11, 11, 12, 12) more times. At the same time, when piece measures 13 (13, 14, 14, 15, 15, 16)" (33 [33, 35.5, 35.5, 38, 38, 40.5] cm) from beg, end with a RS row.

SHAPE ARMHOLE

Next row (WS): BO 7 (8, 8, 9, 11, 11, 13) sts, work to end of row—19 (20, 21, 21, 21, 22, 22) sts rem when all shaping is complete.

Work even until piece measures 21 (21, 23, 23, 25, 25, 27)" (53.5 [53.5, 58.5, 58.5, 63.5, 63.5, 68.5] cm) from beg, ending with a WS row.

BO all sts.

Left Front

CO 36 (38, 40, 42, 44, 46, 48) sts.

Row 1 (RS): *K2, p2; rep from * to last 4 (6, 4, 6, 4, 6, 4) sts, knit to end of row.

Row 2 (WS): P4 (6, 4, 6, 4, 6, 4), *k2, p2; rep from * to end of row.

Rep rows 1 and 2 until rib measures 1" (2.5 cm), ending with a WS row.

Next row (setup, RS): Knit to last 4 sts, work row 1 of cable patt over last 4 sts.

Next row: Work row 2 of cable patt over first 4 sts, purl to end of row.

Note: Read over next section carefully as armhole and front neck shaping are worked at the same time.

Cont as established until piece measures 8 (8, 9, 9, 10, 10, 11)" (20.5 [20.5, 23, 23, 25.5, 25.5, 28] cm) from beg, ending with a WS row.

SHAPE NECK

Next row (dec, RS): Knit to last 6 sts, k2tog, work next row of cable patt over rem 4 sts—1 st dec'd.

Next row: Purl.

Rep last 2 rows 9 (9, 10, 11, 11, 12, 12) more times. At the same time, when piece measures 13 (13, 14, 14, 15, 15, 16)" (33 [33, 35.5, 35.5, 38, 38, 40.5] cm) from beg, end with a WS row.

SHAPE ARMHOLE

Next row (RS): BO 7 (8, 8, 9, 11, 11, 13) sts, work to end of row—19 (20, 21, 21, 21, 22, 22) sts rem when all shaping is complete.

Work even until piece measures 21 (21, 23, 23, 25, 25, 27)" (53.5 [53.5, 58.5, 58.5, 63.5, 63.5, 68.5] cm) from beg, ending with a WS row.

BO all sts.

finishing

Weave in ends. Block pieces to finished measurements. Sew shoulder and side seams.

BELT

Cut 45 pieces of yarn, each about 84 (89, 93, 97, 101, 105, 109)" (2.1 [2.3, 2.4, 2.5, 2.6, 2.7, 2.8] m) long. Holding all strands together, tie an overhand knot 8" (20.5 cm) from one end of group. Anchor knot to a stationary object such as a doorknob. Divide the strands into 3 groups of 15 strands each. Braid strands to last 10" (25.5 cm) or desired length, taking care to keep work even. Tie an overhand knot, leaving 8" (20.5 cm) free. Trim ends to an even length.

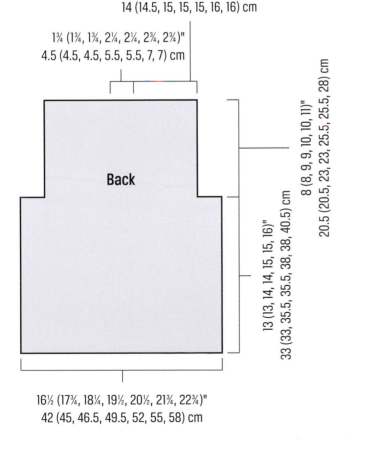

5½ (5¾, 6, 6, 6, 6¼, 6¼)"
14 (14.5, 15, 15, 15, 16, 16) cm

1¾ (1¾, 1¾, 2¼, 2¼, 2¾, 2¾)"
4.5 (4.5, 4.5, 5.5, 5.5, 7, 7) cm

Back

8 (8, 9, 9, 10, 10, 11)"
20.5 (20.5, 23, 23, 25.5, 25.5, 28) cm

13 (13, 14, 14, 15, 15, 16)"
33 (33, 35.5, 35.5, 38, 38, 40.5) cm

16½ (17¾, 18¼, 19½, 20½, 21¾, 22¾)"
42 (45, 46.5, 49.5, 52, 55, 58) cm

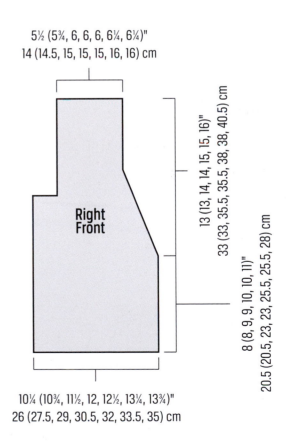

5½ (5¾, 6, 6, 6, 6¼, 6¼)"
14 (14.5, 15, 15, 15, 16, 16) cm

Right Front

13 (13, 14, 14, 15, 15, 16)"
33 (33, 35.5, 35.5, 38, 38, 40.5) cm

8 (8, 9, 9, 10, 10, 11)"
20.5 (20.5, 23, 23, 25.5, 25.5, 28) cm

10¼ (10¾, 11½, 12, 12½, 13¼, 13¾)"
26 (27.5, 29, 30.5, 32, 33.5, 35) cm

here comes the sun
TRIANGLE SHAWL

This cheery shawl is simply shaped to be easily sized up or down to fit different sizes and styles. The stockinette-stitch body is delicately adorned with a gentle picot edging in a contrasting color and yarnover increases.

Designed by Larissa Brown

Finished Size

21" (53.5 cm) deep × 43" (109 cm) across at widest point.

Yarn

Chunky weight (#5 Bulky).

Shown here: Cascade Yarns *Pacific Chunky* (40% superwash merino, 60% acrylic; 120 yd [110 m]/100 g): #12 yellow (MC), 3 skeins; #40 peacock (CC), 1 skein.

Needles

Size U.S. 11 (8 mm): 40" to 60" (100 to 150 cm) circular (cir).

Adjust needle size if necessary to obtain the correct gauge.

Notions

Tapestry needle.

Gauge

12 sts and 19 rows = 4" (10 cm) over St st.

Shawl

With MC, CO 5.

Row 1 (RS): (K1, yo) 4 times, k1—9 sts.

Row 2 and all WS rows: K1, purl to last st, p1.

Row 3: K1, yo, k2, yo, k1, yo, place marker (pm), k1, yo, k1, yo, k2, yo, k1—15 sts.

Row 5: K1, yo, k2, yo, knit to marker, yo, sm, k1, yo, knit to last 3 sts, yo, k2, yo, k1—6 sts inc'd.

Row 6: K1, purl to last st, p1.

Rep last 2 rows 34 more times—225 sts; piece should measure about 20½" (52 cm) from beg along center of shawl.

Change to CC. BO as foll: BO 1, *using cable method (see Glossary) CO 1, BO 3; rep * to end.

finishing

Weave in ends. Block to finished measurements, pinning out each picot point.

Quick & Clever Gifts

Choose from any of these whimsical designs to brighten someone's day. From charming sweaters and contemporary blankets for the modern baby to an ingenious mitten scarf or cushy slipper socks for a favorite friend, or even a treat for yourself, you'll find something for everyone on your list.

rockabye baby
WAVY LACE BLANKET

Knit back and forth in an easy lace pattern with garter-stitch and stockinette details, this quick-to-knit blanket makes an ideal baby shower gift. Worked in a soft blue and green multicolored yarn, it will be at home in any nursery.

Designed by Tanis Gray

Finished Size

34" (86.5 cm) wide × 32" (81.5 cm) long, blocked.

Yarn

Chunky weight (#5 Bulky).

Shown here: Cascade Yarns *Pacific Multi Chunky* (40% superwash merino, 60% acrylic; 120 yd [110 m]/100 g): #616 seamist, 5 skeins.

Needles

Size U.S. 10½ (6.5 mm): 32" (80 cm) circular (cir).

Adjust needle size if necessary to obtain the correct gauge.

Notions

Tapestry needle.

Gauge

11 sts and 17½ rows = 4" (10 cm) over lace chart, blocked.

Blanket

CO 94 sts.

Knit 4 rows.

Work rows 1–12 of lace chart 11 times, or to desired length, ending with a WS row.

Knit 4 rows.

BO all sts kwise.

Finishing

Weave in ends. Block to finished measurements.

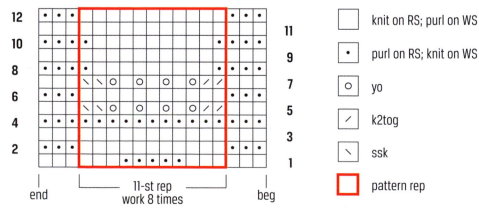

Lace Chart

	knit on RS; purl on WS
•	purl on RS; knit on WS
o	yo
∕	k2tog
∖	ssk
▢	pattern rep

end   11-st rep work 8 times   beg

hugs & kisses
CABLED MITTENS AND HAT SET

What better way to say "I love you" than knitting someone a matching hat and mitten set with an XOXO cable pattern? The cozy mittens are knit in the round and feature garter-stitch cuffs. The charming hat is adorned with garter earflaps, cable and lace details, twisted cording, and pom-poms.

Designed by Robin Melanson

Finished Sizes

Hat: About 17" (43 cm) circumference and 10¾" (27.5 cm) deep from brim to top.

Mittens: About 8" (20.5 cm) hand circumference and 11¼" (28.5 cm) long.

Yarn

Chunky weight (#5 Bulky).

Shown here: Cascade Yarns *Pacific Chunky* (40% superwash merino, 60% acrylic; 120 yd [110 m]/100 g): #37 clover, 3 skeins for both hat and mittens (or 2 skeins for hat or mittens).

Needles

Size U.S. 10½ (6.5 mm): 16" (40 cm) long circular (cir) and set of 5 double-pointed (dpn).

Adjust needle size if necessary to obtain the correct gauge.

Notions

Cable needle (cn); stitch markers (including one in a different color for beg of rnd); waste yarn or stitch holder; tapestry needle; cardboard (for making pom-poms).

Gauges

14 sts and 20 rnds = 4" (10 cm) over St st.

One 8-st cable panel from cable chart = about 1¾" (4.5 cm) wide.

2/2 LC (2 over 2 left cross): Slip next 2 sts onto cn and hold in front of work, k2, k2 from cn.

2/2 RC (2 over 2 right cross): Slip next 2 sts onto cn and hold in back of work, k2, k2 from cn.

GARTER STITCH IN ROWS (ANY NUMBER OF STS)

All rows: Knit.

GARTER STITCH IN ROUNDS (ANY NUMBER OF STS)

Rnd 1: Purl.

Rnd 2: Knit.

Rep rnds 1 and 2 for patt.

Hat

EARFLAP (MAKE 2)

Using 2 dpns, CO 4 sts.

Row 1 (WS): Sl 1 wyf, knit to end.

Row 2 (RS): Sl 1 wyf, knit to last st, M1L, k1—1 st inc'd.

Rep row 2 eleven more times—16 sts.

Work 4 rows even in garter st, ending with a RS row.

Cut yarn, leaving a 6" (15 cm) tail. Set aside.

Rep for second earflap, but work 5 rows even in garter st, ending with a WS row. Do not cut yarn.

BAND

With cir needle and RS facing, cont from sts of second earflap, using cable method (see Glossary) CO 24 sts, turn work, with WS of first earflap facing, k16, turn work, CO 16 sts—72 sts. With RS facing, slip first st on LH needle to cn and hold in front of work, slip last st from RH needle to LH needle, place st on cn onto RH needle, place marker (pm) for beg of rnd. Join for working in rnds, being careful not to twist sts.

Rnd 1: P1, *k2, p2; rep from * to last st, p1.

Rnds 2–4: Rep rnd 1.

Establish patt as foll:

Rnd 1: Remove beg-of-rnd m, work 6 sts in rib, pm for new beg of rnd, *p1, k2tog, yo, p1, pm, k4, p2, work rnd 1 of cable chart over next 8 sts, p2, k4, pm; rep from * twice more, omitting pm at end of last rep.

Rnd 2: *P1, k2, p1, sm, k4, p2, work rnd 2 of cable chart over next 8 sts, p2, k4, sm; rep from * twice more.

Rnd 3: *P1, yo, ssk, p1, sm, k4, p2, work rnd 3 of cable chart over next 8 sts, p2, k4, sm; rep from * twice more.

Rnd 4: *P1, k2, p1, sm, k4, p2, work rnd 4 of cable chart over next 8 sts, p2, k4, sm; rep from * twice more.

Rnds 5–16: Cont patt as established, working rnds 5–16 of chart over cable.

Rep rnds 1–16 until piece measures about 5¼" (13.5 cm) from beg.

SHAPE CROWN

Change to dpns when there are too few sts to work comfortably on cir needle.

Next rnd (dec): *Work to m, sm, ssk, work to 2 sts before next m, k2tog, sm; rep from * to end—6 sts dec'd.

Rep dec rnd every 3 rnds 8 more times—18 sts rem.

Next rnd (dec): (K2tog) 9 times—9 sts rem.

Cut yarn, leaving an 8" (20.5 cm) tail, draw tail through rem sts, and pull tight to close hole.

Finishing

Weave in ends.

TWISTED CORDS

Cut 3 strands of yarn, each about 50" (127 cm) long. Slip group of strands through CO end of earflap, anchor one end of group to a stationary object. Tightly twist strands until cord will double back on itself. Tie ends together and distribute twist evenly, making sure earflap is at center of cord. If desired, knot again and trim close to second knot to adjust length. Repeat for second earflap.

POM-POMS (MAKE 3)

Cut 2 cardboard circles about 3" (7.5 cm) in diameter, with a hole in the center about 1¼" (3.2 cm) in diameter. Cut a narrow wedge out of each circle, so that pieces are C shaped. Hold both circles together and wind yarn around them until center hole is nearly filled. Cut yarn around outer edge, being careful that strands do not fall out of circle. With yarn threaded on a tapestry needle, secure cut strands, working between the two circles, and knot tightly.

Trim top pom-pom to 3" (7.5 cm) diameter, and pom-poms for ends of ties to 2¼" (5.5 cm) diameter. Sew larger pom-pom to top of hat and smaller pom-poms to twisted cords.

Left Mitten

CUFF

With dpns, CO 32 sts. Divide sts evenly over 4 dpn. Pm for beg of rnd, and join for working in rnds, being careful not to twist sts. Work 9 rnds in garter st worked in the rnd, ending with a purl rnd.

Next rnd (dec): (K14, k2tog) twice—2 sts dec'd.

Work 3 rnds even.

Next rnd (dec): (K13, k2tog) twice—2 sts dec'd.

Work 3 rnds even.

Next rnd (dec): (K12, k2tog) twice—26 sts.

Work 4 rnds even, ending with a knit rnd.

HAND

Next rnd (inc): K13, M1L, k3, p1, (k2, M1L) twice, k2, p1, k2, M1L—30 sts.

Next rnd: K17, p1, work rnd 1 of cable chart over next 8 sts, p1, knit to end.

THUMB GUSSET

Rnd 1 (inc): K13, pm for gusset, M1L, k1, M1R, pm for gusset, work to end—2 sts inc'd.

Work 2 rnds even, working new sts in St st.

Next rnd (inc): Knit to first gusset m, sm, M1L, knit to next gusset m, M1R, sm, work to end—2 sts inc'd.

Rep last 3 rnds twice more—38 sts, with 9 sts in thumb gusset.

Work 1 rnd even.

Next rnd: Knit to first gusset m, remove m and place next 9 sts on waste yarn or holder for thumb, remove second gusset m, CO 1 st over gap, work to end—30 sts.

Cont even until piece measures about 7" (18 cm) from top of cuff.

SHAPE TOP

Next rnd (dec): (K1, k2tog) to end—20 sts rem.

Knit 1 rnd even.

Next rnd (dec): (K2tog) to end—10 sts rem.

Rep last rnd once more—5 sts rem.

Cut yarn, leaving an 8" (20.5 cm) tail, draw tail through rem sts, and pull tight to close hole.

THUMB

Place 9 held gusset sts onto dpns, pick up and knit 1 st in gap over thumb, knit to end—10 sts. Pm for beg of rnd, join for working in rnds.

Work even in St st until thumb measures about 2¼" (5.5 cm).

Next rnd (dec): (K2tog) to end—5 sts rem.

Cut yarn, leaving an 8" (20.5 cm) tail, draw tail through rem sts, and pull tight to close hole.

Right Mitten

Work as for left mitten to beg of thumb gusset.

THUMB GUSSET

Rnd 1 (inc): M1L, k1, M1R, pm for gusset, work to end—2 sts inc'd.

Work 2 rnds even, working new sts in St st.

Next rnd (inc): M1L, knit to gusset m, M1R, sm, work to end—2 sts inc'd.

Rep last 3 rnds twice more—38 sts, with 9 sts in thumb gusset.

Work 1 rnd even.

Next rnd: Place 9 sts on waste yarn or holder for thumb, remove gusset m, CO 1 st over gap, work to end—30 sts.

Complete as for left mitten.

Finishing

Weave in ends, using tails to close any gaps at thumb join.

Cable Chart

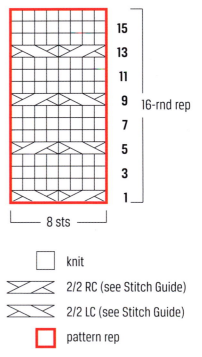

16-rnd rep

8 sts

☐ knit

2/2 RC (see Stitch Guide)

2/2 LC (see Stitch Guide)

☐ pattern rep

sweater girl
RAGLAN CARDIGAN

This pretty-in-pink, top-down baby cardigan is knit with charming cable details and reverse stockinette edgings. With a button at the yoke allowing for an open front without the worry of falling off, this sweater if perfect for the girl on the go.

Designed by Melissa Goodale

Finished Sizes

18¼ (19¼, 20½, 21¼, 22¼)" (46.5 [49, 52, 54, 56.5] cm) chest circumference.

3 (6, 12, 18, 24) months. Sweater shown in size 18 months.

Yarn

Worsted weight (#4 Medium).

Shown here: Cascade Yarns *Pacific* (40% superwash merino, 60% acrylic; 213 yd [195 m]/100 g): #31 rose, 2 (2, 2, 2, 2) skeins.

Needles

Size U.S. 7 (4.5 mm): 24" (60 cm) circular (cir) and set of 4 or 5 double-pointed (dpn).

Adjust needle size if necessary to obtain the correct gauge.

Notions

Cable needle (cn); stitch markers; stitch holders; one ⁹⁄₁₆" (14 mm) button; tapestry needle.

Gauge

18 sts and 24 rows = 4" (10 cm) over St st.

Stitch Guide

3/3 LC (3 over 3 left cross): Slip next 3 sts onto cn and hold in front of work, k3, k3 from cn.

3/3 RC (3 over 3 right cross): Slip next 3 sts onto cn and hold in back of work, k3, k3 from cn.

Rev St st (reverse stockinette stitch): Purl RS rows, and knit WS rows.

Sweater

COLLAR

With cir needle, CO 56 (56, 64, 64, 64) sts.

Row 1 (RS): K2, purl to last 2 sts, k2.

Rows 2 and 4: Sl 1 wyf, knit to last 2 sts, sl 1 wyf, k1.

Row 3: Sl 1 wyf, k1, purl to last 2 sts, sl 1 wyf, k1.

YOKE

Setup row (RS): Sl 1 wyf, k7, p1, knit 2 (2, 3, 3, 3), place marker (pm), knit 8 (8, 10, 10, 10), pm, knit 18 (18, 20, 20, 20), pm, knit 8 (8, 10, 10, 10), pm, knit 2 (2, 3, 3, 3), p1, k6, sl 1 wyf, k1.

Next row (WS): Sl 1 wyf, k1, p6, k1, purl to last 9 sts, k1, p6, sl 1 wyf, k1.

Next row (inc, RS): *Work in patt to m, LLI, sm, LRI; rep from * 3 more times, work in patt to end—8 sts inc'd.

Work 1 WS row even.

Next row (buttonhole, inc): Sl 1 wyf, k1, (put 2 sts just worked back on LH needle, k2) twice, 3/3 LC, *work in patt to m, LLI, sm, LRI; rep from * 3 more times, work in patt to last 8 sts, 3/3 RC, sl 1 wyf, k1—8 sts inc'd.

Work 1 WS row even.

Next row (inc, RS): *Work in patt to m, LLI, sm, LRI; rep from * 3 more times, work in patt to end—8 sts inc'd.

Work 1 WS row even.

Rep last 2 rows twice more—16 sts inc'd.

Next row (cable, inc, RS): Sl 1 wyf, k1, 3/3 LC, *work in patt to m, LLI, sm, LRI; rep from * 3 more times, work in patt to last 8 sts, 3/3 RC, sl 1 wyf, k1—8 sts inc'd.

Work 1 WS row even.

Rep inc every RS row 4 (5, 5, 6, 7) more times, working cable crossing every 8 rows—136 (144, 152, 160, 168) sts.

DIVIDE FOR BODY AND SLEEVES

Next row (RS): Work 21 (22, 23, 24, 25) sts in established patt for left front, place next 28 (30, 32, 34, 36) sts on holder for sleeve, use cable method and CO 5 (5, 6, 6, 6) sts for underarm, k38 (40, 42, 44, 46) sts for back, place next 28 (30, 32, 34, 36) sts on holder for sleeve, CO 5 (5, 6, 6, 6) sts for underarm, work rem 21 (22, 23, 24, 25) sts in patt—90 (94, 100, 104, 108) sts.

BODY

Cont first 8 and last 8 sts in established patt, work St st over rem sts until piece measures 8 (9, 9½, 10, 10½)" (20.5 [23, 24, 25.5, 26.5] cm) from bottom of Collar, ending 4 rows after last cable crossing. Cont in rev St st for 4 rows same as Collar. BO all sts.

SLEEVE (MAKE 2)

With dpn and RS facing, beg at center of underarm CO sts, pick up and knit 3 (3, 4, 4, 4) sts, k28 (30, 32, 34, 36) sts from holder, then pick up and knit 3 (3, 4, 4, 4) sts along rem underarm CO sts—34 (36, 40, 42, 44) sts. Pm for beg of rnd, and join for working in rnds.

Next rnd (dec): K3, k2tog, knit to last 5 sts, ssk, knit to end—32 (34, 38, 40, 42) sts. Work even in St st until sleeve measures 1½" (3.8 cm) from armhole.

Next rnd (dec): K1, k2tog, knit to last 3 sts, ssk, k1—2 sts dec'd.

Rep dec rnd every 9 rnds 1 (1, 2, 2, 2) more time(s)—28 (30, 32, 34, 36) sts. Work even until sleeve measures 5 (5½, 6½, 7, 7½)" (12.5 [14, 16.5, 18, 19] cm). Purl 4 rnds. BO all sts pwise.

Finishing

Weave in ends. Block to finished measurements. Sew button to right front in center of cable opposite buttonhole.

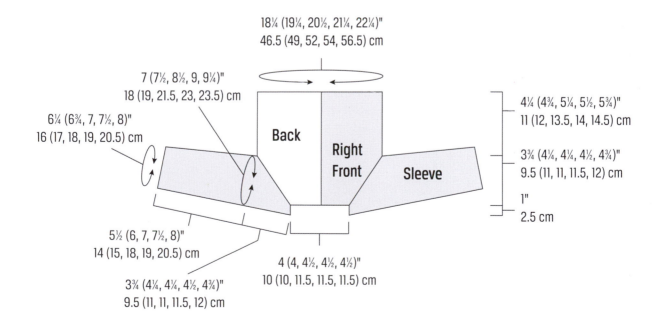

18¼ (19¼, 20½, 21¼, 22¼)"
46.5 (49, 52, 54, 56.5) cm

7 (7½, 8½, 9, 9¼)"
18 (19, 21.5, 23, 23.5) cm

6¼ (6¾, 7, 7½, 8)"
16 (17, 18, 19, 20.5) cm

Back

Right Front

Sleeve

4¼ (4¾, 5¼, 5½, 5¾)"
11 (12, 13.5, 14, 14.5) cm

3¾ (4¼, 4¼, 4½, 4¾)"
9.5 (11, 11, 11.5, 12) cm

1"
2.5 cm

5½ (6, 7, 7½, 8)"
14 (15, 18, 19, 20.5) cm

3¾ (4¼, 4¼, 4½, 4¾)"
9.5 (11, 11, 11.5, 12) cm

4 (4, 4½, 4½, 4½)"
10 (10, 11.5, 11.5, 11.5) cm

our house
INTARSIA PILLOW

This house is a very, very, very fine house! This huggable pillow is knit in one large piece, folded over, seamed at the sides, and buttoned at the back. With a textured roof and grass sandwiching intarsia windows and a button doorknob, it can easily be customized to match your own house or for a thoughtful housewarming gift.

Designed by Amy Bahrt

Finished Size

19" × 26½" (48.5 × 67.5 cm).

Yarn

Worsted weight (#4 Medium).

Shown here: Cascade Yarns *Pacific* (40% superwash merino, 60% acrylic; 213 yd [195 m]/100 g): #33 cactus (A), 1 skein; #13 gold (B), 1 skein; #51 honeysuckle pink (C), 1 skein; #40 peacock (D), 2 skeins; #38 violet (E), 1 skein.

Needles

Size U.S. 7 (4.5 mm) needles.

Adjust needle size if necessary to obtain the correct gauge.

Notions

Tapestry needle; four ¾" (19 mm) yellow buttons; 20" × 26" (51 × 66 cm) pillow form; small amount of fiberfill, yarn scraps, or cotton balls.

Gauge

18½ sts and 26 rows = 4" (10 cm) in St st.

Note

Pillow is knit in one piece, using the intarsia method to change colors. Use a separate ball of yarn for each color area. On every row at at each color change, twist yarns to avoid a hole by laying the strand just worked over the strand to be worked.

Stitch Guide

GRASS PATTERN

Row 1 (RS): Beg with A, knit.

Row 2: Purl.

Row 3: *K4, p2; rep from* to last 4 sts, k4.

Row 4: Purl.

Row 5: Knit.

Row 6: P2, *k2, p4; rep from* to last 2 sts, k2.

Rows 7 and 8: Rep rows 1 and 2.

Row 9: K2, *p2, k4; rep from * to last 2 sts, p2.

Rows 10 and 11: Rep rows 4 and 5.

Row 12: *P4, k2; rep from * to last 4 sts, p4.

Row 13: Knit.

Row 14: Purl.

Row 15: K2, *p2, k4; rep from * to last 2 sts, p2.

Rows 16 and 17: Rep rows 10 and 11.

Row 18: P2, *k2, p4; rep from * to last 2 sts, k2.

Rows 19–21: Rep rows 1–3.

Rows 22 and 23: Rep rows 4 and 5.

ROOF PATTERN

Row 1 (RS): Beg with E, knit.

Rows 2 and 3: Knit.

Row 4: Purl.

Rep rows 1–4 for roof.

GARTER STITCH

Row 1: Knit.

Rep row 1 for patt.

Pillow

With D, CO 88 sts. Work in garter st for 12 rows, ending with a WS row. Work in St st until piece measures 7½" (19 cm) from bottom edge, ending with a WS row.

Join A and work rows 1–23 of grass patt, then work rows 2–11 once more. Knit 1 row on WS for turning ridge. Work rows 1–23 of grass patt, then work rows 2–10 once more.

Next row (RS): Join D and cont in St st as foll: K32, join C and k24, join separate skein of D and knit to end. Cont in St st as established until piece measures about 4" (10 cm) above grass patt, ending with a WS row.

Next row (RS): With D k8, join B and foll 18 sts of chart 1, join separate skein of D and k6, with C k24, with D k6, join B and foll 18 sts of chart 1, join separate skein of D and knit to end. Cont as established through row 22 of chart.

With D only, work in St st for 2¼" (5.5 cm), ending with a WS row.

Next row (RS): With D, k8, join B and foll 18 sts of chart 1, join separate skein of D and k6, join separate skein of B and foll 24 sts of chart 2, join separate skein of D and k6, join B and foll 18 sts of chart 1, join separate skein of D and knit to end. Cont as established through row 22 of charts. With D only, work in St st for 2¼" (5.5 cm), ending with a WS row.

Join E, beg roof patt and work even for 2 rows.

Next row (dec, RS): Ssk, work next row of patt to last 2 sts, k2tog— 2 sts dec'd.

Rep dec row every RS row 15 more times—56 sts rem. Piece should measure about 5" (12.5 cm) from beg of roof patt. Work 1 WS row even.

Next row (inc, RS): K1, M1, work in patt to last st, M1, k1—2 sts inc'd.

Rep inc row every RS row 15 more times—88 sts. Work 1 WS row even.

Join D and work in St st until piece measures 7½" (19 cm) from edge of roof, ending with a WS row.

Work in garter st for 6 rows.

Next row (buttonhole, RS): K21, (BO 2 sts for buttonhole, k20) twice, BO 2 sts, k21.

Next row: Knit and CO 2 sts over each buttonhole gap. Cont in garter st for 4 more rows. BO all sts.

finishing

Weave in ends. Block to finished measurements.

Fold bottom of pillow to WS at turning ridge and top of pillow at narrowest part of shaping (should fold at a purl row), overlapping garter bands with buttonholes on top. Sew side seams along straight and angled edges, working through both thicknesses of overlapped edges. Sew 3 buttons to garter band under buttonholes and 1 button to door as indicated in photo.

Mark top edge of pillow form about 3" (7.5 cm) from each side edge and 5" (12.5 cm) down from top on each side. Draw lines connecting marks on each side. Carefully cut pillow form cover only along lines. Remove small amount of fiberfill from pillow on each side of top. Turn cut edges to inside and whipstitch closed.

Insert pillow form into pillow. Button closed.

CHIMNEY

With C, CO 14 sts. Work in St st until piece measures 3" (7.5 cm). BO all sts. Sew side edges tog. Center seam at back of chimney, then sew top edge of chimney closed.

Lightly stuff with fiberfill, yarn scraps, or cotton balls. Sew bottom edge closed. Sew bottom seam to roof as indicated in photo and tack back of chimney to roof to secure chimney in an upright position.

B

D

Chart 1

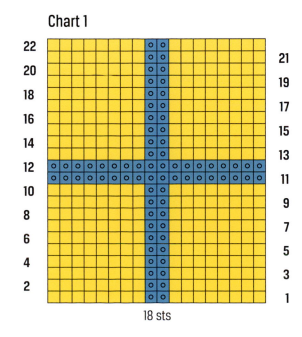

18 sts

Chart 2

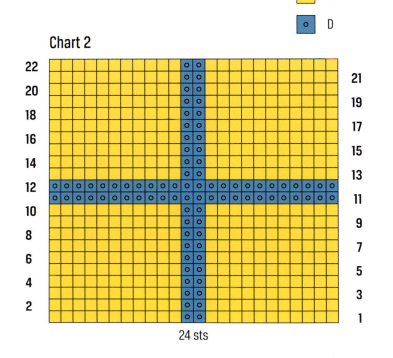

24 sts

climbing vines
CABLED LEG WARMERS

Keep those gorgeous gams warm with these toasty leg warmers knit in the round. One side of each leg warmer features columns of cables and the other seed stitch. Designed to be generous in length, these textured beauties are perfect to wear with a skirt or over skinny jeans.

Designed by Debbie O'Neill

Finished Sizes

About 9½ (11, 12¼)" (24 [28, 31] cm) leg circumference at top, unstretched; 21" (53.5 cm) length. Shown in size 9¼" (23.5 cm).

Yarn

Worsted weight (#4 Medium).

Shown here: Cascade Yarns *Pacific* (40% superwash merino, 60% acrylic; 213 yd [195 m]/100 g): #31 rose, 2 (3, 3) skeins.

Needles

Set of 4 size U.S. 7 (4.5 mm) double-pointed (dpn).

Adjust needle size if necessary to obtain the correct gauge.

Notions

Cable needle (cn); stitch markers; tapestry needle.

Gauge

22 sts and 30 rows = 4" (10 cm) over seed stitch.

2/1 LPC (2 over 1 left purl cross): Sl 2 sts onto cn and hold in front of work, p1, k2 from cn.

2/1 RPC (2 over 1 right purl cross): Sl 1 st onto cn and hold in back of work, k2, p1 from cn.

2/2 LC (2 over 2 left cross): Sl 2 sts onto cn and hold in front of work, k2, k2 from cn.

2/2 RC (2 over 2 right cross): Sl 2 sts onto cn and hold in back of work, k2, k2 from cn.

2/3 LC (2 over 3 left cross): Sl 3 sts onto cn and hold in front of work, k2, sl purl st from cn back onto LH needle, p1, then k2 from cn.

2/3 RC (2 over 3 right cross): Sl 3 sts onto cn and hold in back of work, k2, sl purl st from cn back onto LH needle, p1, then k2 from cn.

K2, P2 RIB (MULTIPLE OF 4 STS)

Rnd 1: *K2, p2; rep from* to end of rnd.

Rep rnd 1 for patt.

SEED STITCH (MULTIPLE OF 2 STS + 1)

Rnd 1: K1, *p1, k1; rep from *.

Rnd 2: P1, *k1, p1; rep from *.

Rep rnds 1 and 2 for patt.

Leg Warmer (make 2)

CO 60 (68, 76) sts. Place marker (pm), and join for working in rnds, being careful not to twist sts. Work k2, p2 rib for 2½" (6.5 cm).

Next rnd (setup): Work 11 (11, 15) sts in seed st, pm, (p2, k4) twice, p2, (p2, k2) twice, M1P, (k2, p2) twice, p2, (k4, p2) twice, pm, work 5 (13, 17) sts in seed st, M1P—62 (70, 78) sts.

Work as foll, beg with row 2 of cable chart (row 1 was worked in the setup rnd):

Rnds 2-32: Work in seed st to m, sm, work cable chart over next 45 sts, sm, work in seed st to end of rnd.

Rnd 33: Work in seed st to m, M1 kwise or pwise to maintain seed st patt, sm, work cable chart over next 45 sts, sm, M1 kwise or pwise to maintain seed st patt, work in seed st to end of rnd—2 sts inc'd.

Rep rnds 2-33 twice more—68 (76, 84) sts. Cont even in established patt until piece measures 2½" (6.5 cm) less than desired length, ending with row 7 or row 15 of cable chart.

Next rnd (setup): P1, (k2, p2) 8 (8, 9) times, k2, p1, p2tog, *k2, p2; rep from * to last 2 sts, k2, M1P—68 (76, 84) sts.

Next rnd: P1, *k2, p2; rep from * to last st, p1. Rep last rnd for 2½" (6.5 cm). BO all sts in patt.

Finishing

Weave in ends. Block if desired.

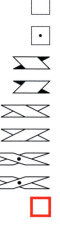

knit

· purl

2/1 LPC (see Stitch Guide)

2/1 RPC (see Stitch Guide)

2/2 LC (see Stitch Guide)

2/2 RC (see Stitch Guide)

2/3 LC (see Stitch Guide)

2/3 RC (see Stitch Guide)

pattern rep

Cable Chart

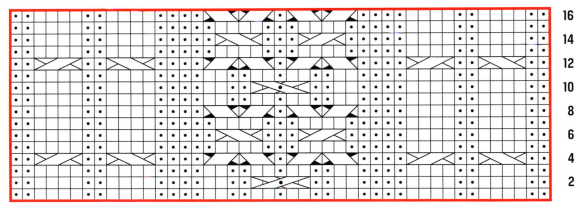

45-st panel

knit to be square
TEXTURED SQUARES BLANKET

A simple combination of knit and purl stitches creates a texture babies will love. The easy-to-follow diamonds-and-squares pattern is framed with a simple seed-stitch border, making this reversible blanket a perfect beginner project.

Designed by Faina Goberstein

Finished Size

About 38¾" × 36" (98.5 × 91.5 cm).

Yarn

Worsted weight (#4 Medium).

Shown here: Cascade Yarns *Pacific* (40% merino wool, 60% acrylic; 213 yd [195 m]/100 g): #29 jade, 6 skeins.

Needles

Size U.S. 5 (3.75 mm): 32" (80 cm) circular (cir).

Adjust needle size if necessary to obtain the correct gauge.

Notions

Markers (m); tapestry needle.

Gauge

21 sts and 29 rows = 4" (10 cm) over textured pattern.

Blanket

CO 203 sts.

Work 6 rows in seed st, ending with a RS row.

Next row (setup, WS): Sl 1, (p1, k1) 3 times, knit to last 7 sts, (k1, p1) 3 times, k1.

Next row (RS): Sl 1, (p1, k1) twice, p2, work 18-st rep of texture patt row 1 to last 16 sts, work last 9 sts of patt, p2, (k1, p1) twice, k1.

Next row: Sl 1, (p1, k1) 3 times, work last 9 sts of patt, work 18-st rep of

texture patt row 2 to last 7 sts, (k1, p1) 3 times, k1.

Cont as established until piece measures 35" (89 cm) from beg, ending with row 13 of chart.

Next row (WS): Sl 1, work next 6 sts in seed st, knit to last 7 sts, work next 6 sts in seed st, k1.

Work 6 rows in seed st, ending with a WS row.

BO all sts pwise.

Finishing

Weave in ends. Block to finished measurements.

Stitch Guide

TEXTURE PATTERN (MULTIPLE OF 18 STS + 9)

Row 1 (RS): *(P1, k1) 5 times, k8; rep from * to last 9 sts, (p1, k1) 4 times, p1.

Row 2: Purl.

Row 3: Rep row 1.

Row 4: P9, *p4, k1, p13; rep from * to end.

Row 5: *(P1, k1) 5 times, k2, (p1, k1) twice, k2; rep from * to last 9 sts, (p1, k1) 4 times, p1.

Row 6: P9, *p2, (k1, p1) 3 times, p10; rep from * to end.

Row 7: *P1, k1; rep from * to end.

Row 8: Rep row 6.

Row 9: Rep row 5.

Row 10: Rep row 4.

Rows 11 and 13: Rep row 1.

Row 12: Purl.

Rows 14 and 16: P8, *(k1, p1) 5 times, p8; rep from * to end.

Row 15: Knit.

Row 17: *K4, p1, k13; rep from * to last 9 sts, k4, p1, k4.

Row 18: P3, (k1, p1) twice, p2, *(k1, p1) 5 times, p2, (k1, p1) twice, p2; rep from * to end.

Row 19: *K2, (p1, k1) 3 times, k10; rep from * to last 9 sts, k2, (p1, k1) 3 times, k1.

Row 20: *K1, p1; rep from * to end.

Row 21: Rep row 19.

Row 22: Rep row 18.

Row 23: Rep row 17.

Rows 24 and 26: Rep row 14.

Row 25: Knit.

Rep rows 1–26 for patt.

SEED STITCH (ODD NUMBER OF STS)

Row 1 (WS): Sl 1, *p1, k1; rep from * to end.

Row 2: Sl 1, *p1, k1; rep from * to last 2 sts, k2.

Rep rows 1 and 2 for patt.

toasty tootsies
SLIP-STITCH SLIPPER SOCKS

These cozy socks work up in a jiffy. A slip-stitch colorwork cuff is knit flat, then folded over and seamed to become the perfect topper to these ribbed slippers.

Designed by Lynn Wilson

Finished Sizes

To fit women's shoe sizes 7–9; about 7–9" (18–23 cm) foot circumference.

Yarn

Chunky weight (#5 Bulky).

Shown here: Cascade Yarns **Pacific Chunky** (40% superwash merino, 60% acrylic; 120 yd [110 m]/100 g): #48 black (A), 1 skein; #33 cactus (B), 2 skeins.

Needles

Size U.S. 10 (6 mm): straight needles and set of 4 or 5 double-pointed (dpn).

Adjust needle size if necessary to obtain the correct gauge.

Notions

Stitch marker; tapestry needle.

Gauge

14 sts and 18 rows = 4" (10 cm) over St st.

Slippers (make 2)

CUFF

With straight needles and A, CO 34 sts. Purl 1 row. Work rows 1–20 of cuff patt, then work row 1 once more. Cut B.

SOCK

Divide sts evenly over 3 or 4 dpns. With WS facing, place marker (pm) and join to work in rnds, being careful not to twist sts. (**Note:** The WS of the cuff is at the right side of the work so that when it is folded down over the sock the RS of the cuff is showing.)

Rnd 1: With A only, ssk, knit to last 2 sts, k2tog—32 sts.

Rnds 2–5: Knit.

Rnds 6–10: Work rib patt. Cut A at end of last rnd.

With B only, cont in rib patt until ribbed portion of the sock measures about 11–12" (28–30.5 cm) or until sock measures 1" (2.5 cm) less than desired finished length. (**Note:** A narrow foot will need less length; a wide foot will need more length.)

TOE

Rnd 1: *K2, p2tog; rep from * to end—24 sts.

Rnds 2 and 3: *K2, p1; rep from * to end.

Rnd 4: *Ssk, p1; rep from * to end—16 sts.

Rnd 5: *K1, p1; rep from * to end.

Rnd 6: Ssk around—8 sts.

Cut yarn, leaving about a 10" (25.5 cm) tail, draw tail through rem sts twice, pull tight to close hole, fasten off on WS.

Finishing

Sew cuff seam using mattress stitch (see Glossary).

Weave in ends. Fold cuff down over sock and block if desired.

Stitch Guide

CUFF PATTERN

Row 1 (WS): With A, purl.

Row 2 (RS): With B, k2, *sl 1 wyb, sl 1 wyf, sl 1 wyb, k1; rep from * to end.

Row 3: With B, p1, *sl 3 wyb, yo, p1; rep from * to last st, p1.

Row 4: With A, knit, dropping all yo's off the needle to make long, loose B strands across RS of work.

Row 5: With A, purl.

Row 6: With B, k2, *sl 1 wyb, insert RH needle under loose strand from row 4, then into next st on LH needle and knit, lift loose strand over st just worked and off needle, sl 1 wyb, k1; rep from * to end.

Row 7: With B, p1, *sl 1 wyf, p1, sl 1 wyf, k1; rep from * to last st, p1.

Row 8: With A, knit.

Row 9: With A, purl.

Row 10: With B, k2, *sl 1 wyf, k1; rep from * to end.

Rows 11–20: Rep rows 1–10, reversing colors.

RIBBING PATTERN

Rnd 1 and all following rnds: *K2, p2; rep from * to end of rnd.

double duty
MITTEN SCARF

It's a scarf. It's a pair of mittens. It's both! You'll never lose a mitten again when you knit this clever accessory that combines two winter essentials. Give a friend a hand and knit another as a gift.

Designed by Galina Carroll

Finished Sizes

Scarf: 61" (155 cm) long × 5¾" (14.5 cm) wide.

Mittens: 10" (25.5 cm) long × 5¼" (13.5 cm) wide.

Yarn

Worsted weight (#4 Medium).

Shown here: Cascade Yarns *Pacific* (40% superwash merino, 60% acrylic; 213 yd [195 m]/100 g): #45 Concord grape (A), 1 skein; #53 beet (B), 1 skein; #51 honeysuckle pink (C), 1 skein.

Needles

Size U.S. 7 (4.5 mm): straight and 32" (80 cm) long or longer circular (cir) needles.

Adjust needle size if necessary to obtain the correct gauge.

Notions

Size E/4 (3.5 mm) crochet hook; tapestry needle.

Gauge

16 sts and 34 rows = 4" (10 cm) over garter stitch.

Note

The scarf is worked using the intarsia method to change colors. Use a separate ball of yarn for each color area. On every row at at each color change, twist yarns to avoid a hole by laying the strand just worked over the strand to be worked.

Stitch Guide

GARTER-STITCH STRIPE PATTERN (ANY NUMBER OF STS)

Rows 1 and 2: With B knit.

Rows 3 and 4: With C knit.

Rep rows 1–4 for patt.

Scarf

With A and cir needle, CO 244 sts. Do not join.

Rows 1 and 2: Knit.

Rows 3 and 4: With B k60, with C k124, with B k60.

Rows 5 and 6: With A k70, with B k20, with C k64, with B k20, with A k70.

Rows 7–11: With B k42, with C k160, with B k42.

Row 12: With A k93, with C k76, with A k75.

Row 13: With A k75, with C k76, with A k93.

Row 14: With B k102, with C k73, with B k69.

Row 15: With B k69, with C k73, with B k102.

Row 16: With A k36, with C k154, with A k54.

Row 17: With A k54, with C k154, with A k36.

Row 18: With A k114, with C k95, with A k35.

Row 19: With A k35, with C k95, with A k114.

Rows 20, 22, and 24: With B k92, with C k37, with B k115.

Rows 21 and 23: With B k115, with C k37, with B k92.

Rows 25 and 27: With A k79, with C k130, with A k35.

Rows 26 and 28: With A k35, with C k130, with A k79.

Rows 29, 31, and 33: With B k78, with C k71, with B k95.

Rows 30, 32, and 34: With B k95, with C k71, with B k78.

Row 35: With A k106, with C k50, with A k88.

Row 36: With A k88, with C k50, with A k106.

Rows 37, 39, and 41: With B k25, with C k123, with B k96.

Rows 38 and 40: With B k96, with C k123, with B k25.

Row 42: With A k186, with C k35 sts, with A k23.

Row 43: With A k23, with C k35, with A k186.

Row 44: With B k114, with C k50, with B k80.

Row 45: With B k80, with C k50, with B k114.

Rows 46–49: With A knit.

BO all sts kwise.

Mittens (make 2)

PALM

Work at both ends of the scarf at once (left and right mitten) or knit 4 pieces separately (2 left, 2 right).

With A and straight needles, pick up and knit 23 sts along one short end of scarf.

Rows 1–9: *K1, p1; rep from * to end of row.

Change to B.

Rows 1–18: Work in garter st stripe patt.

THUMB

Inc row 1: Using knitted method CO 3 sts for thumb, k3 new sts, knit to end—26 sts.

Inc row 2: Knit to last st, M1, k1—1 st inc'd.

Inc row 3: Kfb, knit to end—1 st inc'd.

Rep inc rows 2 and 3 once more, then rep inc row 2 once more—31 sts.

Dec row 1: K6, k2tog, join a second skein of yarn, knit to end—23 sts for hand and 7 sts rem for thumb.

Dec row 2: K23; k2tog, k5—1 st dec'd.

Dec row 3: K2, (k2tog) twice; k23—23 sts for hand and 4 sts rem for thumb.

BO rem thumb sts.

Work even over rem 23 sts for 26 rows, or until hand is about ½" (1.3 cm) short of desired length, ending with a complete stripe.

SHAPE TOP

Next row (dec): (K2tog) twice, knit to last 4 sts, (k2tog) twice—4 sts dec'd.

Rep last row 3 more times—7 sts rem. BO rem sts.

BACK OF HAND

With A and straight needles, CO 23 sts.

Rows 1–9: *K1, p1; rep from * to end of row.

Change to B.

Rows 1–18: Work in garter-st stripe patt.

THUMB

Row 1 (inc): K23, turn, using knitted method CO 3 sts for thumb, turn, knit to end—26 sts.

Row 2 (inc): Kfb, knit to end—1 st inc'd.

Row 3 (inc): Knit to last st, M1, k1—1 st inc'd.

Rep rows 2 and 3 once more, then rep row 2 once more—31 sts.

Row 4 (dec): K23, join a second skein of yarn, k2tog, knit to end—23 sts for hand and 7 sts rem for thumb.

Row 5 (dec): K5, k2tog; knit to end—1 st dec'd.

Row 6 (dec): K23; (k2tog) twice; k2—23 sts for hand and 4 sts rem for thumb.

BO rem thumb sts.

Work even over rem 23 sts for 26 rows, or until hand is about ½" (1.3 cm) short of desired length, ending with a complete stripe.

SHAPE TOP

Next row (dec): (K2tog) twice, knit to last 4 sts, (k2tog) twice—4 sts dec'd.

Rep last row 3 more times—7 sts rem. BO rem sts.

finishing

Weave in ends. Block to finished measurements.

Place second half of mitten over first half, with WS tog (stripes on RS are solid color; see photo). With crochet hook and A, work 1 row of sc around edges of mitten, leaving the ribbed end open.

Make 2 pom-poms for each mitten with A and C, each 2" (5 cm) in diameter as foll: make 2 each with more of color A than C, and 2 each with more of color C than A.

With A, make 4 short twisted cords, each about 6" (15 cm) long. Attach a cord to each pom-pom. Thread end of each cord through third knit stitch from each edge, going from edge toward center, at back of each hand.

Tie both cords with an overhand knot in center of cords. Tie ends with pom-poms.

tilt-a-whirl
LACE AND GARTER AFGHAN

Knit in a simple pattern that only looks complex, this lace throw can be easily sized up for a larger afghan or down for a baby blanket. The knits and purls and increases and decreases naturally tilt the lace and garter rectangles, giving the finished piece a look of organized chaos.

Designed by Therese Chynoweth

Finished Size

42" (106.5 cm) long × 41½" wide (105.5 cm).

Yarn

Worsted weight (#4 Medium).

Shown here: Cascade Yarns *Pacific* (40% superwash merino, 60% acrylic; 213 yd [195 m]/100 g): #61 silver, 6 skeins.

Needles

Size U.S. 10 (6 mm): 24" (60 cm) long circular (cir).

Adjust needle size if necessary to obtain the correct gauge.

Notions

Stitch markers.

Gauge

15 sts and 26 rows = 4" (10 cm) over main pattern stitch.

Note

A circular needle is used to accommodate the large number of stitches. Work back and forth in rows.

Stitch Guide

MAIN PATTERN (MULTIPLE OF 16 STS + 12)

Row 1 (RS): K2, *k8, (yo, k2tog) 4 times; rep from * to last 10 sts, k10.

Row 2: K10, *p8, k8; rep from * to last 2 sts, k2.

Rows 3–12: Rep rows 1 and 2 five more times.

Row 13: K2, *(ssk, yo) 4 times, k8; rep from * to last 10 sts, (ssk, yo) 4 times, k2.

Row 14: K2, p8, *k8, p8; rep from * to last 2 sts, k2.

Rows 15–24: Rep rows 13 and 14 five more times.

Rep rows 1–24 for main patt.

Throw

CO 156 sts. Do not join; work back and forth in rows.

BORDER 1

Row 1 (RS): Knit.

Rows 2 and 4: Knit.

Row 3: K3, (yo, k2tog) to last st, k1.

Row 5: K1, (k2tog, yo) to last 3 sts, k3.

Row 6: Knit.

BODY

Beg main patt as foll: K2, place marker (pm), *k8, (yo, k2tog) 4 times, pm; rep from * to last 10 sts, k8, pm, k2.

Slipping markers as you come to them, cont in main patt until piece measures about 41¼" (105 cm), ending with patt row 11 or 23.

BORDER 2

Rows 1 and 3 (WS): Knit.

Row 2: K1, (k2tog, yo) to last 3 sts, k3.

Row 4: K3, (yo, k2tog) to last st, k1.

Rows 5 and 6: Knit.

BO all sts kwise.

Finishing

Weave in ends. Block to finished measurements, placing pins at points where the edges naturally slant out from body of throw. To exaggerate the points, place pins where edges extend closest to body of throw.

you are my sunshine
CABLED BABY CARDI

This adorable baby cardigan is a cheerful mix of cables, stockinette stitch, and lace. Topped with crocheted button loops and novelty buttons, this sweet cover-up will surely keep your ray of sunshine happy and snug.

Designed by Robin Melanson

Finished Sizes

20¼ (21½, 22¾, 24)" (51.5 [54.5, 58, 61] cm) chest circumference. To fit 6 (12, 18, 24) months. Sweater shown in size 18 months.

Yarn

Worsted weight (#4 Medium).

Shown here: Cascade Yarns *Pacific* (40% superwash merino, 60% acrylic; 213 yd [195 m]/100 g): #12 yellow, 2 (2, 2, 3) skeins.

Needles

Size U.S. 7 (4.5 mm) needles.

Adjust needle size if necessary to obtain the correct gauge.

Notions

Cable needle (cn); stitch markers; tapestry needle; crochet hook size G/6 (4 mm); three ⅝" (16 mm) buttons.

Gauge

21 sts and 26 rows = 4" (10 cm) over St st.

25 sts and 27 rows = 4" (10 cm) over cable and St st stripe patt.

20 sts and 29 rows = 4" (10 cm) over lower body patt.

Back

CO 64 (68, 72, 76) sts.

Setup row (WS): P2 (4, 6, 8), *k2, p4, k2, p5; rep from * to last 10 (12, 14, 16) sts, k2, p4, k2, p2 (4, 6, 8).

Row 1 (RS): K2 (4, 1, 3), [k1, yo] 0 (0, 4, 4) times, k0 (0, 1, 1), *p2, 2/2 RC, p2, [k1, yo] 4 times, k1; rep from * to last 10 (12, 14, 16) sts, p2, 2/2 RC, p2, [k1, yo] 0 (0, 4, 4) times, k0 (0, 1, 1), k2 (4, 1, 3)—80 (84, 96, 100) sts.

Row 2 (WS): P2 (4, 1, 3), [p1, k1] 0 (0, 4, 4) times, p0 (0, 1, 1), *k2, p4, k2, [p1, k1] 4 times, p1; rep from * to last 10 (12, 18, 20) sts, k2, p4, k2, [p1, k1] 0 (0, 4, 4) times, p0 (0, 1, 1), p2 (4, 1, 3).

Row 3: K2 (4, 1, 3), [k1, p1, ssk, k1, k2tog, p1, k1] 0 (0, 1, 1) time, *p2, k4, p2, k1, p1, ssk, k1, k2tog, p1, k1; rep from * to last 10 (12, 18, 20) sts, p2, k4, p2, [k1, p1, ssk, k1, k2tog, p1, k1] 0 (0, 1, 1) time, k2 (4, 1, 3)—72 (76, 84, 88) sts.

Row 4: P2 (4, 1, 3), [p1, k1, p3tog, k1, p1] 0 (0, 1, 1) time, *k2, p4, k2, p1, k1, p3tog, k1, p1; rep from * to last 10 (12, 16, 18) sts, k2, p4, k2, [p1, k1, p3tog, k1, p1] 0 (0, 1, 1) time, p2 (4, 1, 3)—64 (68, 72, 76) sts.

Rep rows 1-4 until piece measures about 5 (5¾, 6¼, 6¾)" (12.5 [14.5, 16, 17] cm) from beg, ending with a row 4 of patt.

Row 5 (RS): P2 (4, 6, 8), *p2, 2/2 RC, p7; rep from * to last 10 (12, 14, 16) sts, p2, 2/2 RC, p4 (6, 8, 10).

Rows 6 and 8 (WS): P2 (4, 6, 8), *k2, p4, k2, p5; rep from * to last 10 (12, 16) sts, k2, p4, k2, p2 (4, 6, 8).

Row 7: K2 (4, 6, 8), *p2, k4, p2, k5; rep from * to last 10 (12, 14, 16) sts, p2, k4, p2, k2 (4, 6, 8).

Row 9: K2 (4, 6, 8), *p2, 2/2 RC, p2, k5; rep from * to last 10 (12, 14, 16) sts, p2, 2/2 RC, p2, k2 (4, 6, 8).

Rep rows 6-9 until piece measures about 9½ (10½, 11½, 12½)" (24 [26.5, 29, 32] cm) from beg, ending with a WS row.

SHAPE SHOULDERS

BO 10 (11, 11, 12) sts at beg of next 2 rows, then 9 (10, 11, 11) sts at beg of next 2 rows—26 (26, 28, 30) sts. BO rem sts.

Left Front

CO 33 (35, 37, 39) sts.

Setup row (WS): Sl 1 wyf, p1, sl 1 wyf, [k2, p5, k2, p4] twice, k2, p2 (4, 6, 8).

Row 1 (RS): K2 (4, 1, 3), [k1, yo] 0 (0, 4, 4) times, k0 (0, 1, 1), *p2, 2/2 RC, p2, [k1, yo] 4 times, k1; rep from * once more, p2, k1, sl 1 wyb, k1—41 (43, 49, 51) sts.

Row 2 (WS): Sl 1 wyf, p1, sl 1 wyf, *k2, [p1, k1] 4 times, p1, k2, p4; rep from * once more, k2, [p1, k1] 0 (0, 4, 4) times, p0 (0, 1, 1), p2 (4, 1, 3).

Row 3: K2 (4, 1, 3), [k1, p1, ssk, k1, k2tog, p1, k1] 0 (0, 1, 1) time, *p2, k4, p2, k1, p1, ssk, k1, k2tog, p1, k1; rep from * once more, p2, k1, sl 1 wyb, k1—37 (39, 43, 45) sts.

Row 4: Sl 1 wyf, p1, sl 1 wyf, *k2, p1, k1, p3tog, k1, p1, k2, p4; rep from * once more, k2, [p1, k1, p3tog, k1, p1] 0 (0, 1, 1) time, p2 (4, 1, 3)—33 (35, 37, 39) sts.

Rep rows 1-4 until piece measures about 5 (5¾, 6¼, 6¾)" (12.5 [14.5, 16, 17] cm) from beg, ending with a row 4 of patt.

Row 5 (RS): P2 (4, 6, 8), *p2, 2/2 RC, p7; rep from * once more, p2, k1, sl 1 wyb, k1.

Rows 6 and 8 (WS): Sl 1 wyf, p1, sl 1 wyf, *k2, p5, k2, p4; rep from * once more, k2, p2 (4, 6, 8).

Row 7: K2 (4, 6, 8), *p2, k4, p2, k5; rep from * once more, p2, k1, sl 1 wyb, k1.

Row 9: K2 (4, 6, 8), *p2, 2/2 RC, p2, k5; rep from * once more, p2, k1, sl 1 wyb, k1.

Rep rows 6-9 until piece measures about 8¼ (8¾, 9¾, 10½)" (21 [22, 25, 26.5] cm) from beg, ending with a RS row.

SHAPE FRONT NECK

BO at beg of WS rows 7 sts once, 3 (3, 4, 5) sts once, 2 sts once, then 1 st twice—19 (21, 22, 23) sts rem.

Work even until piece measures 9½ (10½, 11½, 12½)" (24 [26.5, 29, 32] cm), ending with a WS row.

SHAPE SHOULDER

BO at beg of RS rows 10 (11, 11, 12) sts once, then 9 (10, 11, 11) sts once.

Right Front

CO 33 (35, 37, 39) sts.

Setup row (WS): P2 (4, 6, 8), [k2, p4, k2, p5] twice, k2, sl 1 wyif, p1, sl 1 wyif.

Row 1 (RS): K1, sl 1 wyb, k1, p2, *[k1, yo] 4 times, k1, p2, 2/2 RC, p2; rep from * once more, [k1, yo] 0 (0, 4, 4) times, k0 (0, 1, 1), k2 (4, 1, 3)—41 (43, 49, 51) sts.

Row 2 (WS): P2 (4, 1, 3), [p1, k1] 0 (0, 4, 4) times, p0 (0, 1, 1), *k2, p4, k2, [p1, k1] 4 times, p1; rep from * once more, k2, sl 1 wyf, p1, sl 1 wyf.

Row 3: K1, sl 1 wyb, k1, p2, *k1, p1, ssk, k1, k2tog, p1, k1, p2, k4, p2; rep from * once more, [k1, p1, ssk, k1, k2tog, p1, k1] 0 (0, 1, 1) time, k2 (4, 1, 3)—37 (39, 43, 45) sts.

Row 4: P2 (4, 1, 3), [p1, k1, p3tog, k1, p1] 0 (0, 1, 1) time, *k2, p4, k2, p1, k1, p3tog, k1, p1; rep from * once more, k2, sl 1 wyf, p1, sl 1 wyf—33 (35, 37, 39) sts.

Rep rows 1-4 until piece measures about 5 (5¾, 6¼, 6¾)" (12.5 [14.5, 16, 17] cm) from beg, ending with a row 4 of patt.

Row 5 (RS): K1, sl 1 wyb, k1, p2, *p7, 2/2 RC, p2; rep from * once more, p2 (4, 6, 8).

Rows 6 and 8 (WS): P2 (4, 6, 8), *k2, p4, k2, p5; rep from * once more, k2, sl 1 wyf, p1, sl 1 wyf.

Row 7: K1, sl 1 wyb, k1, p2, *k5, p2, k4, p2; rep from * once more, k2 (4, 6, 8).

Row 9: K1, sl 1 wyb, k1, p2, *k5, p2, 2/2 RC, p2; rep from * once more, k2 (4, 6, 8).

Rep rows 6-9 until piece measures about 8¼ (8¾, 9¾, 10½)" (21 [22, 25, 26.5] cm) from beg, ending with a WS row.

SHAPE FRONT NECK

BO at beg of RS rows 7 sts once, 3 (3, 4, 5) sts once, 2 sts once, then 1 st twice—19 (21, 22, 23) sts rem.

Work even until piece measures 9½ (10½, 11½, 12½)" (24 [26.5, 29, 32] cm), ending with a RS row.

SHAPE SHOULDER

BO at beg of WS rows 10 (11, 11, 12) once, then 9 (10, 11, 11) sts once.

Sleeve (make 2)

CO 26 (26, 28, 30) sts. Work 5 rows in garter st (knit every row).

Next row (inc, RS): K5 (3, 4, 5), *M1, k5 (4, 4, 4); rep from * 2 (4, 4, 4) more times, M1, knit to end—30 (32, 34, 36) sts.

Setup row (WS): P11 (12, 13, 14), pm, k2, p4, k2, pm, purl to end.

Row 1 (RS): Knit to m, sm, p2, 2/2 RC, p2, sm, knit to end.

Rows 2 and 4 (WS): Purl to m, sm, k2, p4, k2, sm, purl to end.

Row 3: Knit to m, sm, p2, k4, p2, sm, knit to end.

Row 5 (inc, RS): K2, M1R, knit to m, sm, p2, 2/2 RC, p2, sm, knit to last 2 sts, M1L, k2—2 sts inc'd.

Rep rows 2-5 seven (seven, eight, ten) more times—46 (48, 52, 58) sts.

Work even until piece measures about 6½ (7, 8¼, 10½)" (16.5 [18, 21, 26.5] cm) from beg.

BO all sts.

finishing

Weave in ends. Block to finished measurements.

Sew shoulder seams. Place marker at side edges of fronts and back 4½ (4¾, 5¼, 5¾)" (11.5 [12, 13.5, 14.5] cm) down from shoulder. Sew in sleeves between markers. Sew side and sleeve seams.

COLLAR

With RS facing, beg at right front neck edge, pick up and knit 17 (17, 18, 19) sts along right front neck, 26 (26, 28, 30) sts along back neck, and 17 (17, 18, 19) sts along left front neck—60 (60, 64, 68) sts. Knit 5 rows. BO all sts kwise.

Mark placement for 3 buttons on left front as foll: 1 below neckband, 1 just above pattern change, and 1 evenly in between.

Make a button loop on right front to correspond to each button marker as foll: with crochet hook, join yarn to front with a sl st, ch 6, work into space where yarn was joined to make a loop, cut yarn, and fasten off on WS.

Sew buttons to left front opposite button loops.

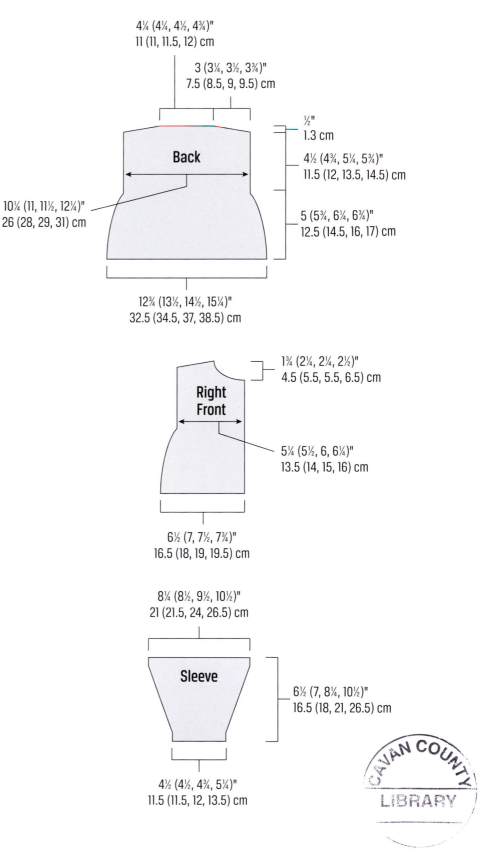

4¼ (4¼, 4½, 4¾)"
11 (11, 11.5, 12) cm

3 (3¼, 3½, 3¾)"
7.5 (8.5, 9, 9.5) cm

Back

½"
1.3 cm

4½ (4¾, 5¼, 5¾)"
11.5 (12, 13.5, 14.5) cm

5 (5¾, 6¼, 6¾)"
12.5 (14.5, 16, 17) cm

10¼ (11, 11½, 12¼)"
26 (28, 29, 31) cm

12¾ (13½, 14½, 15¼)"
32.5 (34.5, 37, 38.5) cm

1¾ (2¼, 2¼, 2½)"
4.5 (5.5, 5.5, 6.5) cm

Right Front

5¼ (5½, 6, 6¼)"
13.5 (14, 15, 16) cm

6½ (7, 7½, 7¾)"
16.5 (18, 19, 19.5) cm

8¼ (8½, 9½, 10½)"
21 (21.5, 24, 26.5) cm

Sleeve

6½ (7, 8¼, 10½)"
16.5 (18, 21, 26.5) cm

4½ (4½, 4¾, 5¼)"
11.5 (11.5, 12, 13.5) cm

abbreviations

beg	begin(ning)		**patt(s)**	pattern(s)
BO	bind off		**pm**	place marker
cir	circular		**pwise**	purlwise, as if to purl
cn	cable needle		**RC**	right cross
CO	cast on		**rem**	remain(s); remaining
cont	continue(s); continuing		**rep**	repeat(s); repeating
dec(s)('d)	decrease(s); decreasing; decreased		**RH**	right hand
dpn(s)	double-pointed needle(s)		**rnd(s)**	round(s)
foll(s)	follow(s); following		**RPC**	right purl cross
inc(s)('d)	increase(s); increasing; increased		**RS**	right side
k	knit		**s2kp**	slip 2 stitches together as if to knit 2 together, knit 1, pass slipped stitches over
k1f&b	knit into the front and back of the same stitch		**sk2p**	slip one stitch, knit 2 stitches together, pass slipped stitch over
k2tog	knit 2 stitches together		**sc**	single crochet
k3tog	knit 3 stitches together		**sl**	slip
kwise	knitwise, as if to knit		**sm**	slip marker
LC	left cross		**ssk**	slip, slip, knit (decrease)
LH	left hand		**ssp**	slip, slip, purl (decrease)
LLI	lifted increase (left leaning)		**sssk**	slip, slip, slip, knit (decrease)
LPC	left purl cross		**St st**	stockinette stitch
LRI	lifted increase (right leaning)		**st(s)**	stitch(es)
m	marker(s)		**tbl**	though back loop
M1	make one (increase)		**tog**	together
M1L	make one (left slant)		**w&t**	wrap and turn
M1R	make one (right slant)		**WS**	wrong side
p	purl		**wyb**	with yarn in back
p1f&b	purl into front and back of same stitch		**wyf**	with yarn in front
p2tog	purl 2 stitches together		**yo**	yarnover
p3sso	pass 3 slipped stitches over			

glossary

Bind-Offs

STANDARD BIND-OFF

Knit the first stitch, *knit the next stitch (two stitches on right needle), insert left needle tip into first stitch on right needle **(Figure 1)** and lift this stitch up and over the second stitch **(Figure 2)** and off the needle **(Figure 3)**. Repeat from * for the desired number of stitches.

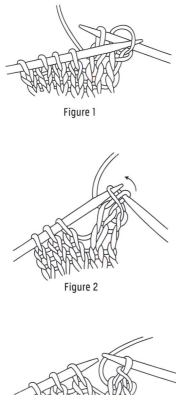

Figure 1

Figure 2

Figure 3

THREE-NEEDLE BIND-OFF

Place the stitches to be joined onto two separate needles and hold the needles parallel so that the right sides of knitting face together. Insert a third needle into the first stitch on each of two needles **(Figure 1)** and knit them together as one stitch **(Figure 2)**, *knit the next stitch on each needle the same way, then use the left needle tip to lift the first stitch over the second and off the needle **(Figure 3)**. Repeat from * until no stitches remain on first two needles. Cut yarn and pull tail through last stitch to secure.

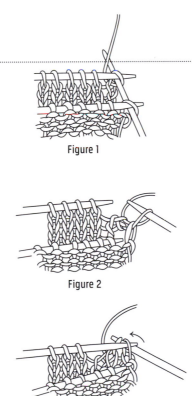

Figure 1

Figure 2

Figure 3

Cast-Ons

BACKWARD-LOOP CAST-ON

*Loop working yarn and place it on needle backward so that it doesn't unwind. Repeat from *.

CABLE CAST-ON

If there are no stitches on the needles, make a slipknot of working yarn and place it on the left needle, then use the knitted method to cast-on one more stitch—two stitches on needle. When there are at least two stitches on the left needle, hold needle with working yarn in your left hand. *Insert right needle between the first two stitches on left needle **(Figure 1)**, wrap yarn around needle as if to knit, draw yarn through **(Figure 2)**, and place new loop on left needle **(Figure 3)** to form a new stitch. Repeat from * for the desired number of stitches, always working between the first two stitches on the left needle.

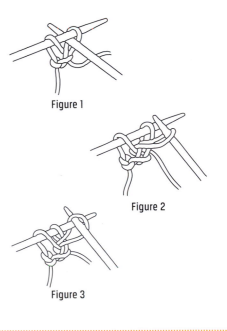

Figure 1

Figure 2

Figure 3

KNITTED CAST-ON

If there are no stitches on the needles, make a slipknot of working yarn and place it on the left needle. When there is at least one stitch on the left needle, *use the right needle to knit the first stitch (or slipknot) on left needle **(Figure 1)** and place new loop onto left needle to form a new stitch **(Figure 2)**. Repeat from * for the desired number of stitches, always working into the last stitch made.

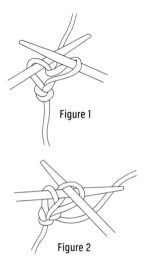

Figure 1

Figure 2

LONG-TAIL (CONTINENTAL) CAST-ON

Leaving a long tail (about ½" [1.3 cm] for each stitch to be cast on), make a slipknot and place on right needle. Place thumb and index finger of your left hand between the yarn ends so that working yarn is around your index finger and tail end is around your thumb and secure the yarn ends with your other fingers. Hold your palm upward, making a V of yarn **(Figure 1)**. *Bring needle up through loop on thumb **(Figure 2)**, catch first strand around index finger, and go back down through loop on thumb **(Figure 3)**. Drop loop off thumb and, placing thumb back in V configuration, tighten resulting stitch on needle **(Figure 4)**. Repeat from * for the desired number of stitches.

Figure 1

Figure 2

Figure 3

Figure 4

TWO-COLOR ITALIAN CAST-ON

Holding two colors together, make a loose slipknot and place on needle. Holding the slipknot tails out of the way, place the dark color (DC) over your left index finger and the light color (LC) over your thumb, as for the long-tail cast-on **(Figure 1)**.

Step 1. To cast on a DC knit stitch, bring the needle tip over the top of LC, under LC, over the top of DC, then under LC and to the front **(Figure 2)**.

Step 2. To cast on a LC purl stitch, bring the needle over both strands, then under both, over the top of LC, and back under DC **(Figure 3)**.

Repeat Steps 1 and 2 **(Figure 4)** for the desired number of stitches, ending with a knit stitch. Drop the slipknot on the first row of knitting.

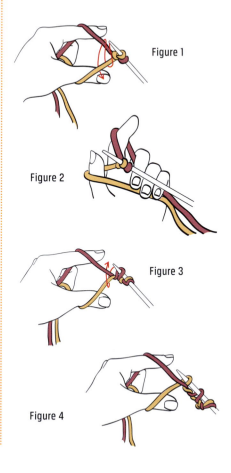

Figure 1

Figure 2

Figure 3

Figure 4

Crochet

SINGLE CROCHET (SC)

*Insert hook into the second chain from the hook (or the next stitch), yarn over hook and draw through a loop, yarn over hook (**Figure 1**), and draw it through both loops on hook (**Figure 2**). Repeat from * for the desired number of stitches.

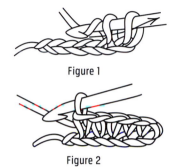

Figure 1

Figure 2

Decreases

KNIT 2 TOGETHER (K2TOG)

Knit two stitches together as if they were a single stitch.

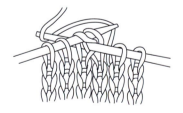

KNIT 3 TOGETHER (K3TOG)

Knit three stitches together as if they were a single stitch.

PURL 2 TOGETHER (P2TOG)

Purl two stitches together as if they were a single stitch.

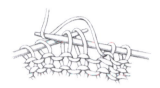

PURL 3 TOGETHER (P3TOG)

Purl three stitches together as if they were a single stitch.

SLIP, SLIP, KNIT (SSK)

Slip two stitches individually knitwise (**Figure 1**), insert left needle tip into the front of these two slipped stitches, and use the right needle to knit them together through their back loops (**Figure 2**).

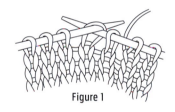

Figure 1

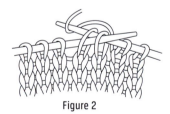

Figure 2

SLIP, SLIP, SLIP, KNIT (SSSK)

Slip three stitches individually knitwise, insert left needle tip into the front of these three slipped stitches, and use the right needle to knit them together through their back loops.

SLIP, SLIP, PURL (SSP)

Holding yarn in front, slip two stitches individually knitwise (**Figure 1**), then slip these two stitches back onto left needle (they will be twisted on the needle), and purl them together through their back loops (**Figure 2**).

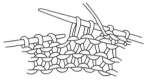

Figure 1

Figure 2

Embroidery

BULLION STITCH

Bring threaded needle out from back to front in the center of a knitted stitch. Leaving a long loop, insert the needle one stitch over, and bring it back out through the center of the initial stitch. Wrap the loop of thread around the needle as many times as desired, then insert the needle back into the same spot it entered before, and pull firmly.

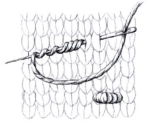

CHAIN STITCH

Bring threaded needle out from back to front at center of a knitted stitch. Form a short loop and insert needle back where it came out. Keeping the loop under the needle, bring needle back out in center of next stitch to the right.

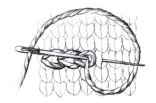

DUPLICATE STITCH

Bring the threaded tapestry needle up from the back at the base of the V of the knit stitch to be covered, then insert it under both loops of the stitch in the row above it, and pull the needle through. Insert the needle into the base of the V again, and pull the needle through to the back of the work.

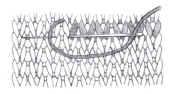

I-Cord (also called Knit-Cord)

This is worked with two double-pointed needles. Cast on the desired number of stitches (usually three to four). Knit across these stitches, then *without turning the needle, slide stitches to other end of needle, pull the yarn around the back, and knit the stitches as usual. Repeat from * for desired length.

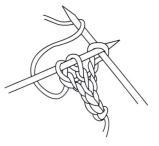

Increases

BAR INCREASE

KNITWISE (K1F&B)

Knit into a stitch but leave the stitch on the left needle (**Figure 1**), then knit through the back loop of the same stitch (**Figure 2**) and slip the original stitch off the needle (**Figure 3**).

PURLWISE (P1F&B)

Work as for a knitwise bar increase, but purl into the front and back of the same stitch.

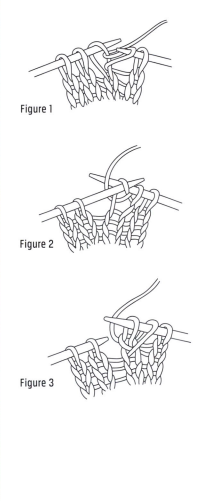

Figure 1

Figure 2

Figure 3

RAISED MAKE-ONE (M1) INCREASE

Note: Use the left slant if no direction of slant is specified.

LEFT SLANT (M1L)

With left needle tip, lift the strand between the last knitted stitch and the first stitch on the left needle from front to back **(Figure 1)**, then knit the lifted loop through the back **(Figure 2)**.

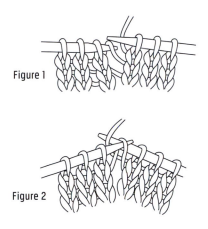

Figure 1

Figure 2

RIGHT SLANT (M1R)

With left needle tip, lift the strand between the needles from back to front **(Figure 1)**. Knit the lifted loop through the front **(Figure 2)**.

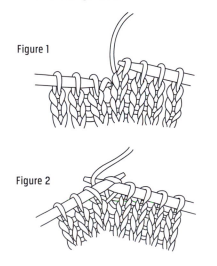

Figure 1

Figure 2

PURLWISE (M1P)

With left needle tip, lift the strand between the needles from front to back **(Figure 1)**, then purl the lifted loop through the back **(Figure 2)**.

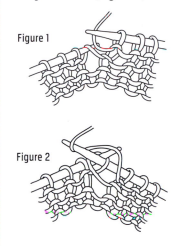

Figure 1

Figure 2

Magic-Loop Technique

Using a 32" or 40" (80 or 100 cm) circular needle, cast on the desired number of stitches. Slide the stitches to the center of the cable, then fold the cable and half of the stitches at the midpoint, then pull a loop of the cable between the stitches. Half of the stitches will be on one needle tip and the other half will be on the other tip **(Figure 1)**. Hold the needle tips parallel so that the working yarn comes out of the right-hand edge of the back needle. *Pull the back needle tip out to expose about 6" (15 cm) of cable and use that needle to knit the stitches on the front needle **(Figure 2)**. At the end of those stitches, pull the cable so that the two sets of stitches are at the ends of their respective needle tips, turn the work around and repeat from * to complete one round of knitting.

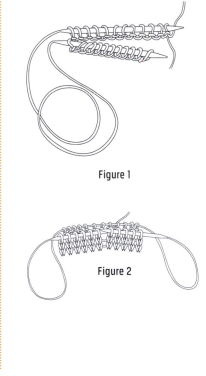

Figure 1

Figure 2

Seams

KITCHENER STITCH

Arrange stitches on two needles so that there is an equal number of stitches on each needle. Hold the needles parallel to each other with wrong sides of the knitting together. Allowing about ½" (1.3 cm) per stitch to be grafted, thread matching yarn on a tapestry needle. Work from right to left as follows:

Step 1. Bring tapestry needle through the first stitch on the front needle as if to purl and leave the stitch on the needle (**Figure 1**).

Step 2. Bring tapestry needle through the first stitch on the back needle as if to knit and leave that stitch on the needle (**Figure 2**).

Step 3. Bring tapestry needle through the first front stitch as if to knit and slip this stitch off the needle. Then bring tapestry needle through the next front stitch as if to purl and leave this stitch on the needle (**Figure 3**).

Step 4. Bring tapestry needle through the first back stitch as if to purl and slip this stitch off the needle. Then bring tapestry needle through the next back stitch as if to knit and leave this stitch on the needle (**Figure 4**).

Repeat Steps 3 and 4 until one stitch remains on each needle, adjusting the tension to match the rest of the knitting as you go. To finish, bring tapestry needle through the front stitch as if to knit and slip this stitch off the needle. Then bring tapestry needle through the back stitch as if to purl and slip this stitch off the needle.

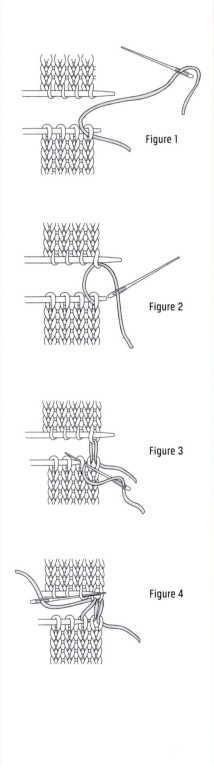

Figure 1

Figure 2

Figure 3

Figure 4

MATTRESS STITCH

Place the pieces to be seamed on a table, right sides facing up. Begin at the lower edge and work upward as follows for your stitch pattern:

STOCKINETTE STITCH WITH 1-STITCH SEAM ALLOWANCE

Insert threaded needle under one bar between the two edge stitches on one piece, then under the corresponding bar plus the bar above it on the other piece (**Figure 1**). *Pick up the next two bars on the first piece (**Figure 2**), then the next two bars on the other (**Figure 3**). Repeat from *, ending by picking up the last bar or pair of bars on the first piece.

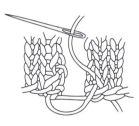

Figure 1

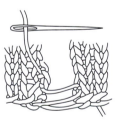

Figure 2

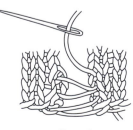

Figure 3

STOCKINETTE STITCH WITH ½-STITCH SEAM ALLOWANCE

To reduce bulk in the mattress stitch seam, work as for the 1-stitch seam allowance but pick up the bars in the center of the edge stitches instead of between the last two stitches.

Short-Rows

KNIT SIDE

Work to turning point, slip next stitch purlwise **(Figure 1)**, bring the yarn to the front, then slip the same stitch back to the left needle **(Figure 2)**, turn the work around and bring the yarn in position for the next stitch—one stitch has been wrapped, and the yarn is correctly positioned to work the next stitch. When you come to a wrapped stitch on a subsequent row, hide the wrap by working it together with the wrapped stitch as follows: Insert right needle tip under the wrap (from the front if wrapped stitch is a knit stitch; from the back if wrapped stitch is a purl stitch; **Figure 3**), then into the stitch on the needle, and work the stitch and its wrap together as a single stitch.

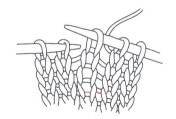

Figure 1

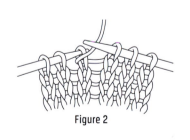

Figure 2

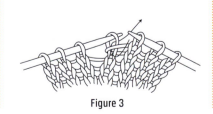

Figure 3

PURL SIDE

Work to the turning point, slip the next stitch purlwise to the right needle, bring the yarn to the back of the work **(Figure 1)**, return the slipped stitch to the left needle, bring the yarn to the front between the needles **(Figure 2)**, and turn the work so that the knit side is facing—one stitch has been wrapped, and the yarn is correctly positioned to knit the next stitch. To hide the wrap on a subsequent purl row, work to the wrapped stitch, use the tip of the right needle to pick up the wrap from the back, place it on the left needle **(Figure 3)**, then purl it together with the wrapped stitch.

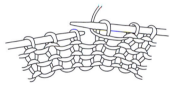

Figure 1

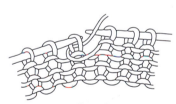

Figure 2

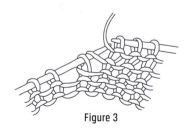

Figure 3

acknowledgments

The saying "it takes a village" is certainly true when it comes to creating a book!

My deepest thanks to diligent editorial director Allison Korleski and to Michelle Bredeson, my extraordinary and hardworking editor. I'm glad we got to work together again!

A hearty thanks to the talented creative team of associate art director Julia Boyles, photographer Joe Hancock, designer Mae Ariola, and production designer Katherine Jackson.

An ardent thanks to my marvelous tech editor Therese Chynoweth.

I'd also like to express my gratitude to the talented designers whose work is featured in this book. It's always an honor to work with such brilliant people who love yarn and knitting needles as much as I do.

index

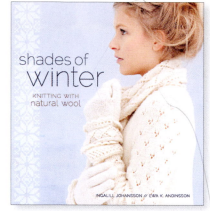
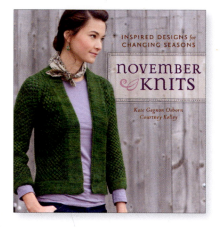